Frank Lloyd Wright

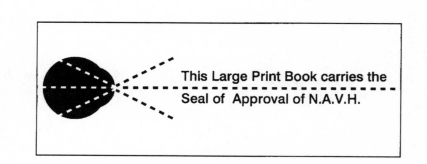

This Large Print Book carries the
Seal of Approval of N.A.V.H.

Frank Lloyd Wright

Ada Louise Huxtable

Thorndike Press • Waterville, Maine

Published in 2005 by arrangement with Lipper Publications
L.L.C. and Viking Penguin, a member of Penguin Group
(USA) Inc.

Thorndike Press® Large Print Biography.

The tree indicium is a trademark of Thorndike Press.

The text of this Large Print edition is unabridged.
Other aspects of the book may vary from the original edition.

Set in 16 pt. Plantin by Elena Picard.

Printed in the United States on permanent paper.

Library of Congress Cataloging-in-Publication Data

Huxtable, Ada Louise.
    Frank Lloyd Wright / Ada Louise Huxtable.
       p. cm. — (A Penguin life)
    "A Lipper/Viking book."
    Large print ed.
    Originally published: New York : Lipper/Viking, 2004.
    ISBN 0-7862-7181-7 (lg. print : hc : alk. paper)
    1. Wright, Frank Lloyd, 1867–1959. 2. Architects —
United States — Biography. I. Title. II. Penguin lives
series.
NA737.W7H89 2005
720′.92—dc22
  [B]   2004058516

Frank Lloyd Wright

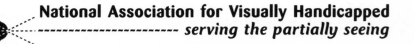
National Association for Visually Handicapped
serving the partially seeing

As the Founder/CEO of NAVH, the only national health agency solely devoted to those who, although not totally blind, have an eye disease which could lead to serious visual impairment, I am pleased to recognize Thorndike Press★ as one of the leading publishers in the large print field.

Founded in 1954 in San Francisco to prepare large print textbooks for partially seeing children, NAVH became the pioneer and standard setting agency in the preparation of large type.

Today, those publishers who meet our standards carry the prestigious "Seal of Approval" indicating high quality large print. We are delighted that Thorndike Press is one of the publishers whose titles meet these standards. We are also pleased to recognize the significant contribution Thorndike Press is making in this important and growing field.

Lorraine H. Marchi, L.H.D.
Founder/CEO
NAVH

★ Thorndike Press encompasses the following imprints: Thorndike, Wheeler, Walker and Large Print Press.

Preface and Acknowledgments

The route to this book has been long and indirect. The project began during a privileged year that I spent as a Director's Fellow at the Dorothy and Lewis B. Cullman Center for Scholars and Writers at the New York Public Library, with the sympathetic encouragement of its founding director, Peter Gay, an experience and opportunity for which I am extremely grateful. Frank Lloyd Wright was not the subject of my fellowship. I was investigating a new and radical kind of architecture based on the use of the computer as a design and production tool, and while I learned a great deal that I needed to know, in a curious way it led me back to an unfinished study on Wright started many years earlier.

I became aware of amazing parallels between Wright's work and the most advanced computer-generated design of today's tech-savvy young architects. Both invented new solutions based on a radical vision and a fascination bordering on obsession with the generating capabilities of geometry. Both pushed inventive fantasy to its limits within the possibilities open to them. They shared the same adventurous mindset, intent on redefining what architecture can do and how it should look. But Wright did it the old-fashioned way, with straightedge, T square, compass, and triangle, everything hand-drawn; he worked with the circles, squares, triangles, and hexagons of solid geometry and the patterns of crystallography. Today's architects, using advanced computer programs, have moved on to fractals and calculus and infinite computational variations for virtually unrestricted shapes and forms. Wright's most important tools were the power of his imagination and his aesthetic sensibilities. Seen in the context of what is happening in architecture in the twenty-first century, his work takes on new significance and meaning.

I continued my research in the library's Frederick Lewis Allen Room the next year, grateful for the hospitality of this treasured writers' sanctuary graciously dispensed by Wayne Furman, and the advantage of the library's art and architecture collections and its enormously helpful staff. The material was organized during a stay at the Medway Plantation in South Carolina, a writers' retreat of stimulating intellectual companionship and sybaritic pleasures, for which I thank its generous guiding spirit, Bokhara Legendre. My constant companions were the boxes of books that traveled with me.

Among those books, the sources I relied on most represent the smallest fraction of the publications on Wright. The bibliography is so large and so accessible — there are books devoted to the Wright bibliography alone — that I am listing only those references that I have found of most recent interest and enduring value for my purposes. An indispensable work was Meryle Secrest's biography *Frank Lloyd Wright* (New York: Knopf, 1992) for its admirably researched account of Wright's life and the new information it added. Brendan Gill's *Many Masks: A Life of Frank Lloyd Wright* (New York: Ballantine, 1987) also provided helpful material. Robert C. Twombly's *Frank Lloyd Wright: An Interpretive Biography* (New York: Harper and Row, 1973) remains one of the best interpretations of Wright's life and art, and Norris Kelly Smith's *Frank Lloyd Wright: A Study in Architectural Content* (New York: Horizon Press, 1966) continues to be of value.

The indispensable scholarly reference is Neil Levine's monumental study, *The Architecture of Frank Lloyd Wright* (Princeton: Princeton University Press, 1996), a significant achievement and important addition to the literature that has been an essential source of detailed history and analysis. Since there is wide discrepancy in the dates given for Wright's buildings, I have taken them from Levine's recent thorough investigations. Grant C. Manson's *Frank Lloyd Wright to 1910: The First Golden Age* (New York: Reinhold, 1958) remains the best account of the early work. Many excellent monographs on Wright's buildings have followed, including those of Joseph Connors, Donald Hoffman, Jack Quinan, Joseph N. Siry, and Kathryn Smith, to name only a few of the authors of these studies, and work by Thomas S. Hines and Narciso Menocal has added depth and detail. I am particularly indebted to Anthony Alofsin's *Frank Lloyd Wright — The Lost Years, 1910–1922: A Study of Influence* (Chicago: University of Chicago Press, 1993) for an invaluable reconstruction of what was previously a black hole in Wright's life and is now revealed as a time of profound importance to his art.

I have used generous selections from

Wright's *Autobiography* because they are so rich and flavorful and eloquently written. Whatever factual slippage they may include, they give us the best sense of the architect and the man. Two memoirs provide additional insights: John Lloyd Wright's *My Father Who Is on Earth* (reissued in 1994 by Southern Illinois University Press) and Edgar Tafel's intimate and affectionate tribute, *Years with Frank Lloyd Wright: Apprentice to Genius* (New York: Dover, 1979). My profound appreciation goes to Bruce Brooks Pfeiffer, director of the Frank Lloyd Wright Archives and vice president of the Frank Lloyd Wright Foundation, for his help, courtesy, and permissions, but especially for the splendid "letters" series he has edited — Wright's correspondence with clients and architects, and the volumes devoted to Wright's exchanges with Lewis Mumford and the progress of the Guggenheim Museum — a remarkably vivid record and fascinating to read.

Providing footnotes for every reference would have made an unwieldy text for a short book, and since its readers are meant to include those who are neither professionals nor specialists, I have avoided footnotes by naming authors directly, wherever their quotations or ideas appear, to give immediate information about the source without interrupting the narrative. The longest quotations are from Wright's *Autobiography*.

My deepest gratitude goes to those who read the manuscript and made helpful suggestions: Karl E. Meyer, editor of the *World Policy Journal* at the New School University in New York, whose opinion I value highly; Professor Thomas S. Hines of the University of California at Los Angeles, whose rich knowledge of Wright and California architecture have been invaluable; and Professor Carol Krinsky of New York University, for her erudite and expert editing and, in particular, for the quality of her questions and the pleasure of her comments. My thanks to all three for kindness that went beyond professional courtesy. And finally, to Joel Honig, the best copy editor, research assistant, and loyal friend that any writer could ever have, who died before this manuscript was completed and whose help and encouragement will be sorely missed; afternoon tea without lively discussions of art and life will be a lonely ritual from now on.

Ada Louise Huxtable
New York City

Introduction

There are two lives of Frank Lloyd Wright: the one he created and the one he lived. The first, his own embellished version, is the standard Wright mythology — the architect as maverick genius and embattled, misunderstood loner, the visionary crusader out of step with ordinary mortals, carrying his banner of "truth against the world" — a character and scenario worthy of a prime-time docudrama. One marvels at the absolute confidence with which Wright manipulated facts to suit the person he wanted, and believed himself, to be. The life as he presented it is, in itself, a creative act.

As more documents and details became available to scholars with the opening of the Frank Lloyd Wright Archives almost thirty years after Wright's death, a series of publications appeared that were devoted to sorting out a long life full of outrageous claims and scandalous behavior. Everything questionable or shameful has been aired in the rush to historical revisionism

13

and psychobiography; the literature is rich in the revelations that prove great artists, like the less gifted, are capable of doing bad things.

The record now stands assiduously and eloquently corrected. The most significant findings, however, are the ones that have increased our understanding of Wright's creative processes. Beyond the determination of what was true and what was false, Wright scholars have been seeking something else — the elusive reality of the extraordinary man who was arguably America's greatest architect, whose work and influence have had an impact on an amazing three centuries of radical change in art, ideas, and technology. Born just after the Civil War into a bucolic horse-and-buggy world, Wright died shortly before his ninety-second birthday, at the start of the Space Age. It is hard to grasp both the length of his career and the extent of the revolution that took place during the six decades of his practice. He never saw an electric light until he went to Chicago as a young man looking for a job. He continued to sharpen by hand the pencils that he used for his delicately colored renderings, as fashions in drawing moved on to the quick bold strokes of the Magic

Marker and slickly impersonal computer-generated images.

The facts of his life are not enough to explain the paradox of an architect who held fast to the nineteenth-century views he grew up with, who clung stubbornly to the romantic moralities of Emerson and Ruskin, while he broke with every convention in his work. How does one reconcile the lifelong embrace of a philosophy already out of date by the early years of the twentieth century with buildings that remain relevant and contemporary, vibrant and alive? Wright's genius — which he proclaimed loudly and often, in what seems less an exaggerated act of bravado as time goes on and history is revisited — remains constant, timeless, and prophetic. Each succeeding generation finds new areas of relevance in his work; he still has lessons to teach.

As the facts emerged, it became clear that reality trumps the mythology being laid to rest. You would not dare invent Wright's life; it is too melodramatic. He survived scandal, murder, fires, divorces, bankruptcy, social ostracism, and pursuit by the FBI for offenses ranging from violation of the Mann Act, for transporting a woman across state lines for immoral purposes (twice, and in the appropriate sequence, each "victim" became his wife), to accusations under the Sedition Act of allegedly encouraging his apprentices to refuse military service during World War II. He lived large and on the edge; to the worst blows of fate he added troubles of his own making. One marvels at the strength and persistence that were required to rebuild his life and practice after each defeat or disaster. He did less well with his personal reputation, but seemed to enjoy and even flaunt his role as outcast and outsider; it becomes clear how necessary that outsize ego really was. At an age when most men retire, he charged into the magnificent creative renaissance of his old age.

By the standards of his contemporaries, he led a shockingly unconventional and thoroughly reprehensible life. He was considered morally and fiscally irresponsible, a view he encouraged with illicit romantic liaisons and perpetually unpaid bills. He made whatever promises and accommodations were necessary as the occasion and his art required. Shame was not an emotion he entertained. He could charm endless advances out of clients' pockets, writing marvelously witty and wheedling letters, while buildings went over budget and out of control. Guile, at the very least, was essential to a lifestyle that was incompatible with solvency, but was also required if he was to build at all. It is hard to realize how strange his work must have seemed in the early 1900s, how unlike anything else and how totally out of step with prevailing taste, how offensive even to conventional neighbors on those suburban lots who considered his houses so peculiar they called them "harems." Clients were scarce and resistant; they had to be as boldly visionary as the architect or be seduced into patronage. He was a master of the art.

The denial of any sources or influences other than his own ideas was one of his most assiduously practiced deceptions. Scholars have established that he was an avid consumer of art and architectural cultures, from pre-history to the avant-garde. We have learned that he was an early, active participant in the exchange of information with his European colleagues, although he maintained throughout his life that he was the sole inventor of modernism. He took an adversarial stand against the International style, in part because he did not share its theories or conform to its doctrinaire principles, but also because dissent suited him so well. He saw

17

himself as the sole possessor and defender of a higher architectural truth, a role he played to the hilt, to the end.

Facts alone are limited in what they can reveal. It takes both the corrected and the doctored versions of the life to give us the full picture of the gifted and fallible person behind the carefully constructed pose and skillfully revised events. What is too easily forgotten is that the art supported by Wright's wiles — whether out of temperament or necessity — has unassailable and enduring integrity. The dismantling of the legend has no effect on this ultimate reality. In the end, art is truth, as sententious as that sounds, or as close to it as we get, and the truth of the man is in the work. The buildings convey the deepest convictions and most authentic expression of the artist; there is nothing duplicitous about them. They tell us the meaning of the life and what it was lived for. This personal view is an attempt to fit the man and his work together through his story, to explore those currents of art and life that he synthesized so brilliantly to change architecture, and how we see it, forever.

1

The life starts with a lie: a changed birth date, from 1867 to 1869, the sort of small, white vanity lie usually embraced by women but common also among men. Like most age changes, it was done later in life. Two years hardly seem worth the trouble for all the chronological complications such things cause. In Frank Lloyd Wright's case, it had the desired effect — it made a case for a precocious talent with an impressively youthful, early success in Chicago in the 1890s, and it kept him shy of the dreaded 90-mark during his brilliant late work in the 1950s. Wright was just two months away from his ninety-second birthday when he died in April 1959, a fact successfully evaded by this small subterfuge. If no one was the wiser, the true date was easy enough to find, once scholars tried. The change did no harm to anyone, although it annoyed his sister Jane all during her lifetime, since it was her birth year that Wright usurped.

There is even some ambiguity about his

name. Family records indicate that he was christened Frank Lincoln Wright when he was born in Richland Center, Wisconsin, on June 8, 1867, although the family name Lloyd seems to have been quickly substituted. Lincoln was one of the most popular names in America at the time, and his mother's family, the Lloyd Joneses, who had come to Wisconsin in search of land and religious freedom as part of the Welsh emigration of the 1840s, were pro-Union and antislavery, like most of the Welsh community. It is not at all unlikely that he bore the name Lincoln briefly in honor of the Civil War president. Frank was one of three children born to Anna Lloyd Wright and William Russell Cary Wright, a widower who brought three children of his own to a troubled marriage that ended in divorce in 1885. Wright's younger sisters, Jane (later known as Jennie) and Maginel (Margaret Ellen, who became Maggie Nell and then Maginel), arrived before Anna denied William her conjugal and domestic services to focus solely on her son, whom she believed to be destined for greatness. From the provision of the right prenatal influences to lifelong support and sacrifice, she dedicated herself to seeing that he achieved it.

The marriage, in 1866, was a late and probably desperate one for Anna, one of ten children born to Richard Lloyd Jones and Mary (Mallie) Thomas Lloyd Jones, who left Wales in 1844 for the promise of cheap, abundant farmland in the American Middle West. Anna was in her midtwenties when she met William, and a thirtieth birthday was not far off, after which she would have been consigned to the common nineteenth-century role of spinster teacher for the rest of her life. Teaching was one of the very few respectable ways a woman could earn a living, and she had been traveling to various Wisconsin communities, riding horseback to country schools, remembered for her abundant dark hair and the brass-buttoned military coat she wore in bad weather. We are told that she was tall and walked freely, like a man.

If Anna needed to marry, William Wright needed a caretaker for his motherless children. A handsome, agreeable man of slight build, with fine, delicate features, he was a gifted musician, orator, and sometime preacher who had been admitted to the bar in 1857. He was warmly received wherever he went, and he moved often. He seems to have left the law to preach at a series of Baptist churches, where he quickly assumed an active social and political role in the community. The local newspaper invariably lauded his talents and social skills, and expressed sincere regret when he departed. The Lloyd Joneses revered education, and William must have appealed to Anna as a man knowledgeable in music, literature, and the law. He was shorter than his wife, who came from a family of tall, physically impressive, abundantly bearded, deeply religious, hardworking farmers and preachers, but what he lacked in stature he made up in erudition and charm.

After making his peripatetic way from New England in 1859, William had settled in Wisconsin with his first wife, Permelia, who died shortly after giving birth to their third child. Anna was teaching school in the area and boarding with the family at the time; the death of William's first wife evidently opened the door to romance, or at least to opportunity. The marriage was to take Anna and a household that grew to six children to New England and back again through a series of failed ambitions and doomed pastorates — McGregor, Iowa, in 1869, Pawtucket, Rhode Island, in 1871, and Weymouth, Massachusetts, in 1874, and back to Madison, Wisconsin, in 1877. It did not help the marriage that the 1870s was a time of deep national depression, which meant the pastor was often unpaid. But with all of his talents, William was apparently unable to make a living; he could neither earn nor handle money. Frank recalled a house often without cash or food, where parishioners of whatever apparently bankrupt church William currently headed would hold "donation parties" that yielded pathetically little. He claimed to remember one that left nothing but twenty-nine pumpkin pies. Each congregation would beg William not to go, and the next place would prove no better.

The return to Wisconsin was probably encouraged and helped by Anna's family, now comfortably established on profitable small farms around Hillside and Spring Green, on the Wisconsin River. Anna rejoined the tight-knit family of the Uncles and the Aunts, as they were known, who would make up the young Wright's world. Life had made the Uncles cautious, practical men. The family's slow, hard journey from Wales to the Middle West had been marked by poverty, hunger, and tragedy, interrupted and delayed by the need to work along the way. One young child fell ill and died en route and had to be buried along the roadside in an unknown grave. Those stern, industrious Welshmen must have found William's misfortunes hard to excuse or to bear. After the family's return from Weymouth, Uncle James drove his wagon the forty miles from his farm to the Wright house in Madison, with a cow tied behind, "so Anna's children could have good fresh milk." Turning to the faith of the Lloyd Joneses, Unitarianism, William received an appointment to a Unitarian church, but the position proved no more successful than the others. In today's critical assessment, and no doubt in the minds of the Uncles, William was a loser, and Anna would be better off without him.

The marriage lasted about seven more stress-filled years, worsening as William retreated into despair. "Failure after failure added to failure," Wright wrote in his *Autobiography*, led to an "inveterate and desperate withdrawal . . . into the arid life of his studies, his books, and his music, where he was oblivious of all else." The retreat no doubt also served as a refuge from his alienated wife, who was neither patient nor long suffering as she saw her dreams disappear. Frank was eighteen when the break finally took place. The conventional wisdom and the Wright mythology, supported by Wright's own account, have maintained that William abandoned Anna. The court records of the divorce, found in Madison by historian Thomas S. Hines and published in the *Wisconsin Magazine of History* in 1967, the centenary of Wright's birth, tell a different story. When the Lloyd Joneses realized that the marriage could not be salvaged, they offered to support Anna and the children if William would leave. Hardly in a position to argue, he agreed to give Anna the house and furnishings and go away; he may even have been secretly relieved.

These proceedings yield Wright's real birth date, which is confirmed by census records and high school documents, and a sad and sordid account of domestic discord. Court documents reveal that it was William who instigated divorce proceedings against Anna, detailing years of what he described as spousal abuse. It was William who claimed to be the deserted partner. Not only had Anna refused to share his bed — "for two years she has protested against and refused me intercourse as between husband and wife" — but she also "wanted more money than I could furnish." In any discussion of their desperate finances she would become "violently angry," and if the beleaguered William objected to her extravagance (although one wonders, under the circumstances, how extravagant she could be), "she would resent any questions about economy." Other wifely duties were withheld. "A large part of my mending I did myself or carried away because when I requested her to do anything it was often neglected . . . [or] when it was done, often threwn [*sic*] in my face or on the floor. . . . She told me 'I hate the very ground you walk on.' " With Anna's admission "that she had no love for her husband," the court concluded that "all of the allegations of the complaint are true." It would have been an extraordinary ploy for William to invent these demeaning hardships in order to be free.

Clearly, Anna made her husband miserable and behaved abominably. But even a kinder, more understanding woman would have been driven to exhaustion and desperation by the unstable household, the constant lack of resources, the unrelieved poverty and anxiety that she could see ahead of her for the rest of her life. Anna was an educated, ambitious woman, with literary and cultural aspirations far above domestic drudgery. She had been trapped in the domestic trivia of raising six children with endless mind-numbing and backbreaking work, without any compensating comfort or security, in abject and constant need. Charm, music, and fine oratory were not enough. She obviously hated her life; stressed beyond endurance, she frequently lost control. William's mending must have been the last straw in a day of escalating chores. Although her actions speak to something cold, and even cruel, in her nature, she was clearly bitterly disappointed in her marriage and unwilling to add more children to the brood. When move after move failed to improve their condition, even hope seemed futile. What was really inexcusable — beyond the violence, or the way she treated her husband and the children — was her championship of her children against his from his first marriage, and her single-minded devotion to her son. From the time he was conceived, she made up her mind that he would be an architect. She hung the right pictures, played the right music, and thought the right thoughts to influence the unborn child. He would deliver her from the despair and hardship of her life, make up for her thwarted ambitions; they would have a golden future together.

In his account of the breakup of the marriage, written years later, after his mother's death, Wright accepted her claim of abandonment, although he had to have been keenly aware of what was really going on. Her version was probably the only acceptable story at a time when a divorced woman's place in society was somewhere between polite ostracism and total disgrace. If he knew the truth, why didn't he tell it, almost a decade after she was gone? Was the memory of a deeply disturbed and obviously unhappy childhood too painful to revisit? Whatever his motivation, it seems unlikely that he would have willingly revealed those traumatic early years. Forms had to be observed and reputations mattered; the time had not yet come for popular soul-bearing confessions and poisonous, mommy-dearest revelations. When he wrote about the divorce in the *Autobiography*, he said "that he never got the heavy thing straight." This was probably not the calculated evasion that some have made it out to be. The children of acrimonious divorce carry a load of conflicted loyalties, of grief and guilt; they never get "the heavy thing straight." He let his mother's story stand, consciously no doubt, and perhaps opportunistically as well; it would also be the most acceptable one, and he reinforced it with his own claim of alienation from his father.

The truth, as usual, was more complex. In that home, dominated by the mother's anger and resentment, it would have been difficult or foolhardy to take sides. Favored and protected by his mother, he could not have forged a close and lasting bond with a father who sought refuge from his wife's abuse by retreating from his family. The Lloyd Joneses had closed ranks to rescue Anna from a failed marriage; it would have been unthinkable for him to stand alone against them. There was no question about where his loyalties lay. William left with only his clothes and his violin, and there was never any contact between father and son again.

After the divorce, William seems to have been in perpetual motion, moving back and forth, from Nebraska to Missouri and Iowa, and finally to the home of a son by his first marriage, near Pittsburgh, where he died in 1904. In the last part of his life, he passed through twenty towns and seven states. The children of his first family remembered a sweet and cheerful man reduced to depression and despondency with the continuous downward spiral of his life.

Those who saw Anna as the unfortunate victim of a bad marriage dismissed him as a self-centered dreamer pursuing personal fulfillment. It is more likely that he was a charming and impractical man whose real virtues and abilities lay in the music and literature he loved, pursuing an elusive livelihood in an unremunerative profession in hard times, with none of the survival skills later perfected by his son. When William was buried in Wisconsin with his first wife, Frank did not attend the funeral; it is known, however, that he made solitary visits to the grave in later years. One can read in Wright's memoirs the mixed memories of the father who grew more remote, the two joined only by the music they shared.

But Frank was clearly William's son. He had his father's fine looks and his small stature — he always claimed 5 feet 8½ inches, which may have been a stretch (he was closer to 5 feet 7 and occasionally wore built-up heels). His easy charm came from his father, and so did his musical ability and abiding love of music. He told the tale of pumping an organ, to the point of total exhaustion, while his father played on, unconscious of the son's fatigue — his carelessness with the boy the source of another fight with Anna. Whatever else was lacking in his youth, and it was almost everything, there was always a piano, and for Frank, in the future, there would always be a piano — in Tokyo during the construction of the Imperial Hotel, in the Arizona desert at his winter camp, in the suite at the Plaza hotel that he kept in New York when he built the Guggenheim Museum.

One suspects that the breadth of his sensibilities as an artist, photographer, and designer of furniture, graphics, books, and all the elements of his buildings, his patronage of Chinese and Japanese art, his obsession with every aspect of his surroundings, his dedicated collecting of beautiful things, owed much to his father, who could never afford more than the books to which he retired in defeat. Wright could not afford these things either — his resources were always subsumed by his self-indulgences — but he bought anyway, running up debts with lordly unconcern. He would use his fees to buy works of art instead of paying his bills. The financial brinkmanship that the son displayed throughout his life equaled and surpassed his father's economic woes, but he made extravagance an art form.

Wright's relationship with his mother

was one of mutual dependence; she would accept his transgressions, tolerate his lapses, and stay close to him until she died. He makes the repeated observation that she always "understood." When an overactive imagination led to an invitation to schoolmates for a party that existed only in his own mind, she made instant molasses candy and produced popcorn and cookies. Later, there would be tacit and total acceptance of far more serious indiscretions. She bought the land for the first Taliesin, the home built for his mistress after he abandoned his wife; her generosity brought him back to the family valley, and the house he would build there would inevitably have a place for her. She tolerated and lived with subsequent mistresses and wives. She traveled to Japan in her eighties to care for him when he was ill, even though he had another woman by his side. He could count on her sympathy when the rest of the world considered him an outcast. She was always there, through guile, persistence, uncritical devotion, and sheer determination — that eternal motivational mix called mother love. She co-opted his loyalty through single-minded possessiveness and support.

He must have been deeply affected by

the insecure, impoverished, unhappy household of his childhood, although he describes evenings around the piano during the Madison years, before the divorce, laughing and singing the Gilbert and Sullivan songs that were then the rage. In his *Autobiography*, he walks a careful line between describing the trials and hardships of a seriously troubled home, and painting a warm picture of old-fashioned nineteenth-century family pleasures. But there is a less attractive account of family life given by William's daughter by his first marriage, Elizabeth, who called Anna a cruel and abusive stepmother. She tells in her diary of a horrifying experience, when Anna, standing at the stove, hit and burned her in a fit of anger, and of being rescued, screaming, by her father. The children he brought with him were eventually sent to his relatives for care. Anna's tantrums were severe enough for William to make inquiries to her family about her mental condition. Some later observers believe that she was emotionally unstable, and the severest of her critics, Wright biographer Brendan Gill, was convinced that she was slightly mad. Given her temperament, frustrated ideals, and the stresses of an emotionally and financially doomed marriage, it is more likely that she was driven into bitter and furious rages through disappointment and unrelenting fatigue.

This gives us some reason to believe that Wright's presentation of a patient, sainted mother as guardian angel of his future — pursuing prenatal architectural influences by putting tastefully oak-framed engravings of English cathedrals on his nursery walls in her determination that he should become an "Architect" (always capitalized in the *Autobiography*, but so is "Mother") — was romanticized and embroidered with willful hindsight by her son. That is, if she did any such thing; it has been suggested by those busily engaged in questioning the legends of his life that it would have been more likely, at that time and in those straitened circumstances, that the newborn's cradle would simply have shared the parents' room, and Edgar Kaufmann Jr., whose father commissioned Fallingwater, Wright's masterpiece of the 1930s, the great house over the waterfall in the Pennsylvania woods, questioned whether there would have been any money for frames. The pictures could have been cut from the easily available *Harper's Weekly*. But the scholarly rush to "truth" underestimates

Anna: she would have managed the frames — Frank remembered framed pictures in his boyhood homes — and arranged for her son to have his own space. Let her have the cathedrals; she probably found a way.

After the family returned to Madison, Anna apparently decided that her son's carefully nurtured artistic sensibilities might have gone a bit overboard. Unlike the large, robust Lloyd Jones men, Frank was a small, solitary child content to read, draw, listen to music, and "make things," daydreaming and following his own pursuits. Although she had encouraged his aesthetic interests, dressed him in velvet suits, and cried when she cut off his curls, she may have had some fears for his masculinity, or at least felt that even an Architect needed a bit of hard work and a dose of reality. When he was eleven years old, she decided a little corrective therapy was needed. The Uncles were consulted and a solution was found; Frank would spend his summers helping on Uncle James's farm. As Uncle James noted, the boy "had as much muscle as a blackbird's got in his leg."

At the time, Frank dreaded and despised those summers; his memories were of backbreaking tasks and he recoiled from the gross aspects of animal husbandry. While there was much solace in the fields and woods, where he would steal time until recalled to his tasks, he found farm life demeaning and distasteful. For the next five summers, he endured what he described as a living hell of hard work, where he learned to "pile tired on tired," as he was constantly required to do by rigorous Lloyd Jones standards, "adding it again . . . and again." He would count the days until September and his return to Madison and school. But he developed work habits and stamina that stayed with him; in his fifties, and even in his eighties, he would exhaust his young staff, urging them to "pile tired on tired." For the rest of his life, he would refer to himself as a farmer, although he would see to it that the farm he established at his Wisconsin home, Taliesin, was worked by others; the live-in apprentices of the Fellowship he established in the 1930s, who paid for instruction in the great man's studio, also labored and brought forth the crops, while he rode grandly by on horseback, the epitome of the gentleman landowner.

He described the detested summer routine with almost total recall more than forty years later in the *Autobiography*. But let him tell it himself — he does it so well. He wrote in the third person, but the tone is intensely immediate throughout. He would arrive at the farm, to be installed in the same white attic room with one small window, heated by a stovepipe from below. At four in the morning: "Sharp rapping on the stovepipe — loud. Again, sharper, louder," and he would reach for the work clothes Uncle James provided, dressing to the rapping on the stovepipe — "a hickory shirt, blue-jean overalls with blue cotton suspenders, coarse blue cotton socks, clumsy cowhide shoes with leather laces" — the shoes and a hated hat soon discarded. A quick splash to his face with water in a basin drawn from a cistern by a bucket tied to a rope, and off to the barn, "where he dutifully began milking as shown, until his hands ached," and "the strange smells sickened him."

He learned the hazards of country life — the cows that "would lean over and crush the breath out of you against the wall of the stall. Beating them over the back with the milking stool only made them push harder." Bare feet in fresh cowpats. Washing the manure off the teats, pinging the milk into the pail, with an occasional spurt to the mouth, as taught by the hired man. Then breakfast, farm plentiful and revolting to the fastidious young aesthete. "Potatoes, fried. Fried cornmeal mush, fried pork, green cheese and cornbread. Pancakes and sorghum. Buttermilk and milk. Coffee and tea, but not for him." Watching the "red-faced, yellow-haired hired man pour sorghum over his big piece of fat pork" would take his appetite away. He remembered the hired man's name — Gottlieb. And with all the milk, there was never any cream.

Next, feeding the calves with Aunt Laura — "teaching the crowding, pushing, bunting things to suck the milk by holding the fingers in the pail . . . a nasty business." Then "carrying sticks of wood to the cross-cut saw." Dinner — "boiled fresh beef, boiled potatoes, carrots, turnips, homemade bread and butter, jam, pickles, prunes, sorghum, honey, green cheese, pie or cake." Afternoon — "holding the split oak rails while Uncle James nailed them to the fence-posts, hands full of slivers, going off to get the cows for the first time, at five. Home to supper at six. Fried potatoes, as regularly as the sun set. Homemade bread and butter. Cornbread, cornmeal mush, milk, honey, homemade preserves. Fried salt pork or smoked beef, creamed." After supper, milking again. "In bed, about half-past seven, too tired to move.

"Again the outrageous banging on the stovepipe . . . the clothes sweat-stiffened. They went on stiff and stayed stiff . . . until limbered up by working in them. . . . Endless, the care of the animals, horses, cows, pigs, sheep." Currying and brushing the workhorses, cleaning the stables "under and behind them," hitching and unhitching them, "putting them to the plow, harrows, seeders, markers, plankers, planters, cultivators and lumber wagons"; "hauling fodder and boiling something . . . for the hogs . . . getting the heavy sows off their own little pigs," alerted "by the infernal, heart-rending squeals. . . . Sickened as you assisted at butchering by seeing the knife stuck deep in the fat-throat and the hot blood gushing and steaming from the one marked for family 'pork.' The smell of their yard — devastating!" Hens: "getting pecked by the lousy things. Getting covered with lice from them . . . striking off the heads of superfluous young roosters when their turn came to be eaten . . . throwing the flapping, convulsive fowl aside in its headless tumble over wood-pile and door-yard in frantic letting go of life. . . ."

The harvesting of the grain, the bundling, hauling, and pitching of the hay, the rhythm of the motions still felt and described: "Aching muscles in the morning." And then there were the mosquitoes "to pester him, and the flies to torture the cows. Cut-grass and nettles and poison ivy. And wasps and bumble bees. Hidden sticks and stumps to stub one's toes. Quicksand in the streams. And hornets' nests in the barn rafters."

But there were also other things to learn, as he fetched the cows, so tired that he hung on to the one with the longest tail, or cut through meadows, or stole time in the woods. "He knew where the lady-slippers grew, and why . . . he could lead you surely to where Jack-in-the-Pulpit stood in the deep shade of the wood, to wild strawberries in the sunny clearings of the hills. To watercress in the cool streams flowing from hillside springs. He knew where the tall red lilies could be found afloat on the tall meadow grass. . . . The choke cherry with its pendent blooms and black clusters of cherries that puckered your throat. . . . The white birches gleaming. Wild grape in bloom festooning the trees and fences. Sumach with its braided foliage and dark red berry-cones. Herbs, and dripping leaves in rain. In the fields, milkweed blossoming, later scattering its fleece on every breeze. The sorrel reddening the fields. . . ." And the boy things: "He would go catching sleek frogs or poking stupid toads. Catching crazy grasshoppers. Listening at night to the high treble of the frog-song. He delighted in devils' darning needles, and turtles, too."

He evokes the sounds, sights, colors, beauty, and wonder of the summer world with an elegiac pleasure almost worthy of the Whittier or Lowell his mother read to him. But being Wright, he cannot resist turning it all into gorgeous grist for the future Architect: "He was studying unconsciously what later he would have called 'Style.' " And then, blending nature into architecture, making that connection between the physical and natural worlds with Olympian certainty and fuzzy abandon, "the boy was some day to learn that the secret of all the human styles in architecture was the same that gave *character* to trees."

He ran away twice, brought back once by Uncle Enos, sent to look for him, to whom he poured out his tearful tale of fatigue, pain, and anguish, and once by Uncle James. He would hide in the hay barn all night while they called for him, feeling gratified and guilty to have turned his suffering into someone else's concern. His mother visited, and cried.

And then Sunday, blessed Sunday — "salvation for the 'tired to tired' week." A bath on Saturday night, water carried from the cistern, part heated on the stove. In the morning, he would put on his city clothes. The Aunts and Uncles would be seated in rockers on the platform of the small, shingled wooden family chapel, its pulpit covered with a cloth of purple velvet and wildflowers gathered by the children. They would have gone out early to bring back a wagon box full of branches of Frank's choosing. It was his delight to display them — "broad masses of blooms and verdure freely arranged, pretty much as they grew . . . only more so."

Wright never forgot the pleasure of those Sundays at church and the solidarity of family life — going to the still cool woods in the early hours to gather those "tremendous riches" to place on the altar, a display indelibly entwined with a family at worship together. The memory was enhanced by the picnics that followed, each family wagon filled with baskets that carried far more than the standard daily fare: stuffed chickens, hard-boiled eggs, corn on the cob to be roasted, sandwiches and pickles, fresh tomatoes, cucumbers to be eaten in the hand with salt, sugared doughnuts, turnovers, cookies, gingerbread, and pies and cakes of all kinds. "Bright colored cloths would be spread on green grass in some cool selected spot . . . in the shade of beautiful trees . . . always near a spring or stream," where the fresh milk would be set to cool.

Half a century later, Wright would call for picnics at Taliesin; the apprentices who spent as much time in the kitchen as at their drafting boards were expected to spread out the same kind of sumptuous repast on the same kind of gaily colored cloths, in the same meadows and hills, in nostalgic homage to the pleasures of childhood and family life, although Wright himself was never a good family man, and the way of life he recalled was gone forever.

2

From the time Anna returned to her family,
Frank knew where his loyalties lay; he became part of the austere and righteous Lloyd
Jones clan. He came to know and love all the
configurations of the family land. His first
work as a youth was to assist the architect of
a new family chapel, and his first building as
a professional was for the Hillside Home
School established and run by the Aunts.
Later, he added a windmill to the school, a
small, bravura design, which he named
Romeo and Juliet for its two structurally adventurous, romantically embracing parts. Although the Uncles vehemently opposed its
unconventional design and never stopped
predicting its collapse, it outlasted them all.

His values — conservative, moralistic,
deeply old-fashioned, emphatically individ-
ualistic — came directly from the Lloyd
Jones family, and they were values
common to the Welsh settlers of the area.
Clannish and devout, they shared a
prideful sense of uniqueness, of "other-

ness." Unlike most immigrants, the Welsh did not spread out widely — the farmers went to Wisconsin and the miners to Pennsylvania — nor did they hasten to learn English or local customs, or seek absorption into the American mainstream. They remained a small, close-knit entity surrounded by much larger immigrant groups of Germans and Scandinavians. Many were Unitarian dissenters from the Church of England who had been persecuted as heretics for their unorthodox beliefs. They did not join the local churches. They built their own chapels, around which the farming families clustered in close communities, where sermons and hymns survived in the Welsh language, Cymric, well into the twentieth century. They were abolitionists and prohibitionists who stressed rectitude, independence, and personal freedom. They also brought with them an anti-British bias, which Wright absorbed and retained, in a more reflexive than reasoned fashion, through the two world wars.

The story of the Welsh in Wisconsin has been told by the historian Phillips G. Davies, who details the ways in which the federal government encouraged occupation and cultivation of the land. Under the preemption laws of 1841, which allowed settlers to claim land in surveyed areas of the new west where they already lived, or planned to locate — it was possible to purchase 160 acres for $1.25 an acre and an $18 registration fee. Two hundred dollars could provide a firm stake in the American future. The later Homestead Act of 1862, which offered settlers up to 160 acres on even more generous terms, continued to encourage westward expansion. The Welsh chose land that reminded them of home, and they gave their farms Welsh names, such as Pen y Daith (end of the journey), or Bryn Mawr (big hill). The Lloyd Joneses acquired several farms in the Helena Valley in Wisconsin's Iowa County, which they owned closely and conspicuously — "the Valley of the God-Almighty Joneses," Wright's sister, Maginel Wright Barney, called it in her memoir in later years.

The Lloyd Joneses had been leaders of a breakaway Unitarian sect in Wales, and they brought both their nonconforming faith and a conviction of their special position in the spectrum of right and wrong to the New World. Wright never lost his belief in the uniqueness and sanctity of his views, and he always managed to rationalize his own lapses from accepted norms.

He could, and did, compose self-justifying statements that explained serious breaches of conduct, like the desertion of his first wife for another woman, in the most elevated terms and with the greatest of ease. His behavior was "honest"; he refused to honor "hypocritical" conventions. He simply created his own moral code.

At some point, the family had adopted a motto, "truth against the world," and it was clear that they stood together in the understanding that some higher truth had been vouchsafed to them alone, by some higher power, which united them against the follies and misdeeds of the weaker members of a less enlightened society. That founding faith, the conviction that they were the possessors and guardians of some special wisdom or vision, was one of the touchstones of Wright's life and the basis of many of his pronouncements and actions in later years. Forging his own way to the truth, against ignorance and reaction, sure that his possession and defense of the truth was not only exclusive but aesthetically and morally correct, became an act of sublime arrogance, long before attitude was an accepted vehicle of social exchange. As he put it, in one of his most famous statements, he made the choice at an early age between "hypocritical humility and honest arrogance." He chose arrogance and never looked back. It was an arrogance fed by his faith in his own gifts and intolerance of lesser talents, and for those whose thinking did not parallel his own. In later years, it congealed into a calculated confrontation with the world, a witty and deliberately outrageous contrariness, with a flagrant disregard for facts, which he manipulated shamelessly.

By birth, background, and temperament, Wright was uniquely suited to the radical cultural climate of his youth. His early years intersected with a revolution in the arts, a time of exalted creativity and fervent artistic reform devoted to the overthrow of the established order and the rejection of the models of the past. The last part of the nineteenth century was the high point of the romantic revolt against eighteenth-century rationalism, and the ideas he would hold for the rest of his life were radical romantic ideas. Rational certitudes of the kind sought by the Age of Enlightenment, the argument of the nineeenth-century thinkers went, allowed for no inspirational or unexpected discoveries. True enlightenment — the meaning of art and life — was to be sought through instinct and subjective personal experience rather than through the rule of reason. By opening oneself to nature and the forces behind it, truth and beauty would be revealed with a new spiritual intensity.

The Lloyd Joneses were as devout in their belief in the cultivation of the mind as in their religious convictions, and they were keenly aware of the intellectual ferment that was moving from the East Coast to the new frontier. They read not only the Bible, but also the work of Lowell and Longfellow; Anna read the poems to the children during the years in Weymouth, when she was close to Concord and the arbiters of American intellectual life. She managed, even with her limited resources, to buy and send back to Wisconsin the books of William Ellery Channing, Theodore Parker, and Thoreau.

It was the writings of the era's most respected literary hero, Ralph Waldo Emerson, however, that inspired Wright. Emerson's full-throttle romanticism bursts from his famous 1836 essay, *Nature*, an evangelical interpretation of man's relationship to the natural world that was read for decades after it appeared. In one of the most famous passages in American literature, Emerson describes an intense emotional epiphany, a transfiguring experience of finding oneness with the universe through nature: "Standing on the bare ground, my head bathed by the blithe air and uplifted into infinite space, all mean egoism vanishes. I become a transparent eyeball. I am nothing. I see all; the currents of the Universal Being circulate through me; I am part and parcel with God." This vision, Emerson believed, could be experienced only in solitary communion with nature. Thus was Thoreau driven into the wilderness. More than a century and a half later, in the age of the transparent navel, with all consciousness turned inward, it is hard to imagine the power of these ideas.

At the epicenter of this intellectual movement were the New England transcendentalists, who preached a quasi-religious nature worship that combined the sublime and the divine in a mystical trinity of nature, spirit, and God. There were bold social experiments like Brook Farm in Massachusetts and New Harmony, Indiana, where a spiritually sanctioned socialism was practiced. John Ruskin and William Morris were the arbiters of an aesthetic avant-garde that embraced the natural over the artificial; Ruskin rejected the Academy and Morris rejected the Machine. From Wordsworth in England to Whitman in America, a passionate and florid literary style celebrated nature and imbued it with an overarching and instructive morality.

Because the Lloyd Jones women were teachers, it is not surprising that Anna had returned from a trip to Philadelphia for the Centennial Exposition of 1876 to the house in Weymouth (she seems to have managed some life of her own) fired by the discovery of the Froebel "gifts" — the wooden blocks, pegs, and brightly colored papers of the advanced kindergarten method of the popular German educator Friedrich Froebel — or that she saw their possibilities for the future Architect. In a much quoted passage from the *Autobiography*, Wright describes "the strips of colored paper, glazed and 'matt,' remarkably soft brilliant colors. . . . The structural figures to be made with peas and small straight sticks . . . the smooth shapely maple blocks with which to build, the sense of which never afterward leaves the fingers . . . and the exciting cardboard shapes with pure scarlet face — such scarlet! . . . What shapes they made naturally if you let them."

Wright repeatedly credited these educational toys as the generators of his architectural forms. In his account of Wright's early years and work, Grant Manson makes a plausible and important case for the architect's fascination with triangles and pinwheeling plans as a result of this youthful indoctrination. Recent revisionist studies have expressed skepticism about the miracle of that early epiphany, since Froebel's methods had been in use in the United States as early as the 1850s, and Anna, an experienced teacher, probably would have already known all about them. But Wright's description of the revelation is irresistible. A later investigation, by Jeanne S. Rubin, concludes that not only was Anna already familiar with the materials and method, but she was also expert in their use. Rubin shows how Anna went beyond the elementary toys called "gifts," to the next level of Froebel's training, providing Frank with the series called "occupations," which carried the experience of seeing to more complex experiments with the geometry of form. Froebel's "kindergarten," a name that was to become synonymous with preschool activities, was meant to include older students; Frank would have been nine, and well able to appreciate and deal with the lessons the material contained.

Rubin's most revealing finding is that Froebel had been a crystallographer before he became an educator, and that all of the forms and the ways in which they were to be used are based on the science of crystallography. One sees this source throughout Wright's career, in his use of the rotated plan, the flipped mirror image, the hexagonal module, buildings designed in series as typical crystal chains. He returned more and more to the lessons and principles learned from the "gifts" and the "occupations," far beyond the sensuous memory of the smooth wooden blocks in his hand, in the sophisticated geometry of his later work. Where geometry stopped, imagination took over. The forms that grew bolder and more fanciful were derived in large part from Froebel's crystallography-based examples. With the disappearance of the strict modernist rules and restrictions against which his late work had been measured, these buildings prefigure the virtually unlimited potential of the computer-generated forms that have seduced the imagination of twenty-first-century architects.

But it was Emerson's and Ruskin's ideas that were the philosophical source of Wright's "organic architecture," which has been dismissed by many as meaningless mysticism, or at best left open to any kind of interpretation. Like Emerson and the transcendentalists, Wright believed in the natural world as the source of physical and spiritual fulfillment. The virtues of nature and the relationship of nature, art, and morality — concepts that were inseparable in the nineteenth-century mind — appear over and over in Wright's pronouncements. Organic architecture, by his own definition, was a way of building "naturally," "in the nature of materials," to unite man and his built world with nature, the human spirit, and the universe. To make an organic, or natural whole, of the concept, the building, and its execution, the nature of the land must be the generator of the architect's work. This union of nature and self, which informed all of Wright's thinking, was an ideal communicated with poetic and inspirational grandeur by the nineteenth century's most influential artists, writers, and philosophers. However vague and pedantic all this became in his redundant declarations, and however hopelessly dated these ideas would seem in the age of machine art and cool rationalist architecture, Wright's philosophy translated into a warmth and beauty in his finest work and an intuitive connection between his buildings and their settings that remain timelessly satisfying.

He read Ruskin from an early age, the books given to him by his mother and the Aunts. The Ruskinian worship of the natural landscape formed his taste and that of several generations. Ruskin relegated man-made intrusions, including the entire Renaissance and the classical tradition, to architectural purgatory; he excepted only the Italian Gothic churches and ruins that suited the romantic frame of mind. Artists and writers painted and wrote in search of the awesomely "sublime."

What Wright does not tell us, or even hint at, are the other ideas and models that shaped the nature of his art. To maintain his Olympian position as the self-described inventor of modern architecture, he could admit to no other interest or influence, or acknowledge any work but his own. We know now that he was an omnivorous reader, in part to compensate for an erratic education, and that he was an avid collector of the latest books and periodicals on art and architecture. He was intensely aware of everything that was going on and immediately receptive to it; he never doubted his own role as an active participant in a period of great creative change. He did not miss a nuance or beat of what was happening abroad. Scholars have established that there was a free flow and exchange of ideas between Europe and America during the vital period that tied the nineteenth and twentieth centuries together. The fashionable British publication *The International Studio* brought Wright the fin de siècle domestic architecture practiced in England by C. F. Voysey, M. H. Baillie-Scott, Philip Webb, and Richard Norman Shaw, a protomodern style of crafted simplicity. He knew the art nouveau of Charles Rennie Mackintosh in Scotland, and was familiar with the seductive charms of the Vienna Secession. He was an admirer of Josef Olbrich's Secession Building and Otto Wagner's Postal Savings Bank in Vienna, and of Peter Behrens's buildings in Berlin. Later, he formed lasting friendships with C. R. Ashbee in England and H. Th. Wijdeveld in the Netherlands, both pivotal figures of developing European modernism.

Historian Anthony Alofsin's investigation of Wright's contacts with the early European avant-garde has convinced him that Wright was familiar with much more than he ever acknowledged. Alofsin's sleuthing has uncovered a treasure trove of examples and contacts. Wright was apparently familiar with the system of mathematical analysis employed by the innovative Dutch architect Hendrik Berlage, in whose studio a generation of architectural activists were trained. He was no stranger to abstraction as it was developing on the Continent; he found it more sympathetic than Louis Sullivan's elaborate foliate ornament, which he abandoned early. It is not inconceivable that he knew the paintings of the synthetists, precursors of the symbolists, who sought a unity of form, color, and meaning by reducing objects to flat patterns of unmodulated color, much as he treated his own decorative detail. The new theories and movements were the subject of articles in the international art press, which he saw regularly. Architects have famously sensitive antennas for the other arts, and for the work of their peers.

Japonisme, a major nineteenth-century taste that affected almost everything visible, movable, wearable, or fashionable, undoubtedly led Wright to Japanese art and the woodblock prints that became so much a part of his own art and life. His career as a dealer in Japanese prints — his collection was a lifelong love affair and essential source of income — has been documented by historian Julia Meech, who found prints sold to the Metropolitan Museum of Art in New York in the 1920s by one F. L. Wright. His introduction to the architecture of Japan by the Ho-o-den, the Japanese pavilion at the 1893 Chicago World's Columbian Exposition, is well known, but it is less well known that he owned a copy of the 1896 edition of Friedrich Deneken's *Japanische Motive für Flächenverzierung*, with its plates of chrysanthemum, peony, and bamboo patterns suitable for transfer to fabrics and pottery.

Ruskin's belief that the correct practice of the arts must recognize and reinforce its moral qualities — moral precepts are the stated principles of his widely read *Seven Lamps of Architecture* — and Morris's concept of art as a social and democratic act led to the late nineteenth century's conflation of the moral and aesthetic that was at the heart of Wright's philosophy. His abstract shapes and stylized natural forms were always endowed with the overarching symbolism dear to the Victorian age's morally elevated principles. The square, for example, was believed to symbolize integrity; Wright adopted the square for his signature in a field of Cherokee red, the Native

American color he favored and married to his memory of the bright, flat red of the Froebel "gifts." The square was the basis of the design of an important early work, Unity Temple, built in Oak Park in 1905–1908, which Thomas Beeby has analyzed to show how Wright's architectural geometry and spiritual symbolism interact. The familiar hallmarks of his style were established early; what is less well understood — and contradicts the popular Wright mythology — is how they evolved within the framework of the nascent modernism that transformed the twentieth century.

The aesthetic movement was already a force for change in Wright's childhood; it decreed a new era of enlightened, artistic design and home decoration. The reforms it preached — and "reform" is the key word for all these nineteenth-century trends embraced in the name of social and aesthetic progress — were transmitted to Wright in the way Anna furnished her homes; he always remembered light-filled rooms with waxed maple floors and cream-colored net curtains hanging straight at the windows, the pictures in narrow maple frames, flowers, leaves, or branches arranged in clear glass vases so the natural pattern of the leaves and stems would show. None of Wright's own interiors were ever without these containers filled with seasonal gatherings.

The fashionable houses of the wealthy patrons who set progressive trends had large entry halls that featured huge hearths and inglenooks, with art glass and pottery tastefully displayed on the many-shelved, mirrored mantels above the fireplaces or on dining room sideboards and plate rails. Oriental rugs were flung diagonally across tables and on bare floors, with romantic landscapes or sentimental genre paintings displayed on easels. The rallying cry of the aesthetic movement, "art for art's sake," was meant to be an antidote to the materialism of the Industrial Revolution and its mass-produced excesses, a purifying act devoted to the elimination of Victorian clutter and the cultivation of taste and beauty. Oscar Wilde carried a lily in its cause. As a young architect, Wright was not averse to lace-trimmed velvet suits. Early photographs show him as the very model of the gentleman artist at the aesthetic cutting edge, hair slightly longer than commonly worn, sporting flowing ties and clothes of his own design. He favored scarfed hats and pantaloons for foreign travel, and booted, country tweeds for rural wear.

William Morris's arts and crafts movement had moved quickly from England to the United States, where reform groups like the Roycrofters, headed by Elbert Hubbard, were in their ascendancy, and the furniture and crafts of Gustave Stickley were in great demand, along with vast numbers of earth-toned pots embraced by whiplash flowers or left virtuously plain. Simple forms, natural materials, and honest joinery were given higher meaning — salvation from the sins of vulgar Victorian display for those who would be converted, and many were. Art and virtue made a heady aesthetic brew. Froebel's lessons were preliminary to everything else Wright learned and embraced and used and reused, as he absorbed radical ideas and shifting styles, transforming them all, in some magical way, into an art of his own. He credited nothing, of course, except his God-given creativity.

He would expound his romantic, Emersonian philosophy for the rest of his life, in an increasingly didactic, pseudo-Whitmanesque prose that would have made the Emersonian eyeball glaze over. But there is also much lucid, beautiful writing in his revealing, provocative, and maddeningly misleading *Autobiography*, where he describes the places he worked and lived with a wonderful vividness and vivacity, and a poetry of their own. He loved the landscape of his birth with a lasting passion. He would build his home and studio on a gently rolling site across the Wisconsin River from the other family holdings, naming it Taliesin after a Welsh poet and mystic, translated as Shining Brow for the position of the house on the side of a hill. Wright would survive tragedy and disasters there, the murder of a lover and her children, desperate financial crises, and three destructive fires, rebuilding each time. No matter where he went or in what cosmopolitan circles he moved, these were his roots. He always came home.

3

Truth is in the mind of the believer. By the time Wright set down his own version of the truth in the *Autobiography* published in 1932, his account had developed an anecdotal consistency, an independent reality. After doing basic research in archives in Madison, the historian Thomas S. Hines concluded that Wright "had no conception of 'truth' as most people define it. . . . His unique creative nature demanded and conceived for himself a *persona,* a mythic personality surrounded by a partially mythic world." His version of events seemed "more appropriate and acceptable as an introduction to his life."

Having lied about his birth, therefore, he also lied about his education; he succumbed to that most common of all sins of vanity after lowering one's age, the inflated educational record. How many, before and since, have doctored their résumés, fudged their transcripts, or invented degrees in the desire to impress or excel? These are the most universal of lies, told by many lesser mortals. If he was an indifferent student who seems never to have finished high school and stayed only briefly in college, inconvenient facts he glossed over and amplified, he would declare that conventional education was worthless to someone with his exceptional sensibilities. He professed to remember nothing from school, since it had nothing to give him. In a family that revered education, he was virtually self-educated; he read widely and was a diligent apprentice and quick learner in the offices where he began his career.

His early schooling is hazy while the family was on the move, although Anna obviously paid close attention to essential skills and uplifting texts. She was able to get him into a private school somewhere along the way. Beyond the introduction of the Froebel "gifts" and poetry readings at home, she also managed at some point to secure one of the refined cultural niceties of the day — oil painting lessons taken from a Miss Landers (Wright seems never to have forgotten a name), who provided "suitable" subjects for canvases that he scorned as "innocent crimes to which an innocent mother had allowed her innocent son to become an innocent party," although he kept "a cardboard cock-robin on a lead pipe branch looking nowhere" in his room in the Madison house.

One has the sense that the opportunities and amenities Anna secured for her son — she seems to have pulled strings quietly and energetically — were provided at a considerable personal price. Even in the food the impoverished family ate, the message of selfless sacrifice came through: when the occasional chicken in the henhouse was killed for dinner, she professed to little appetite and a preference for the neck. Her son must have maintained lifelong feelings of obligation for her saintly self-denial.

The uncomfortable mix of gratitude and guilt was already established when his parents separated, reinforcing the loyalty and self-interest that made him take his mother's side. He remembered his father in music and the books he left behind. He tells how he listened as a child, in bed at night, to his father playing Bach and Beethoven with such passion that the music seemed to reveal mysteries to his young mind about art and life. Thomas S. Hines relates how his oldest son, Lloyd, also listened, in bed at night, to his own father playing the same music "as if his heart would break." Like his father, Wright would insist that his children all learn to play a musical instrument, and the tradition of family musicales continued with the young apprentices at Taliesin.

After the return to Madison, young Frank went to the Second Ward Grammar School, and then to Madison High. Records show that he was an uneven and undistinguished student — good and poor grades in physics, poor to average in algebra, average in rhetoric and botany, a failing algebra grade with the remark "put back" — and there is no indication that he was ever graduated. But he was reading; in elementary school, he secretly devoured the notorious Nickel Library, the "greasy, worn and torn" copies of the blood-and-guts adventures of *Deadeye Dick* and *The Terror of Deadman's Gulch* circulated until found and destroyed by a teacher or parent. Later, the Aunts gave him Ruskin's *Seven Lamps of Architecture*, and Goethe's *Wilhelm Meister* novels; they were also the source of his copies of Ruskin's *Stones of Venice* and *Modern Painters*. He would read books from his father's library — Plutarch's *Lives*, and Carlyle's *Sartor Resartus*. He acquired Viollet-le-Duc's *Discourses on Architecture*, a volume he continued to recommend to his apprentices for many years.

Anna's status had changed from beleaguered wife to needy single parent. As the son, and oldest of the children, Wright had to find work, and his mother seems to have produced a job for him; he was hired in 1885 as a part-time assistant by Allan D. Conover, a practicing civil engineer and professor of engineering at the University of Wisconsin–Madison, for thirty-five dollars a month. Although Wright's duties in Conover's office were at the entry level, this gave him his first lessons in engineering. It seems likely that Conover encouraged him to enroll as a special student in civil engineering at the university, since it is reasonably clear that the young man had neither the grades nor the high school diploma for regular matriculation. This meant going to class in the morning, working for Conover in the afternoon, and studying in the evening.

Or so he wanted us to believe. We have two scenarios again, the real and the doctored, the truth and the supertruth — perhaps the best word for the spin Wright put on facts. He claimed that he spent three and a half years at the university. Never one for the small lie or simple evasion, he was boldly specific in describing "the University training of one Frank Lloyd Wright" as a "freshman, sophomore, junior and part senior — the almost complete course of study ended with the willful abandonment of a diploma at the last moment. He "ran away," he said, in the spring of 1888, just short of receiving the degree, because his courses were without relevance to anything he cared for in the real world. He was too impatient to enter that real world, he explained, to wait for a pointless piece of paper. In the 1950s and '60s, biographers Grant Manson and Finis Farr found a lack of correlation in the university's archives between the school's records and Wright's account. Not three and a half years, but less than two and a half semesters comprised his total university tenure. With that record of poor attendance and nonachievement in both high school and college, he would be called a dropout today — and would not be the first gifted rebel to take that route. Thus he created and embraced his role of independent, nonconforming outsider whose personal search for knowledge and self-realization left conventional learning in the dust.

Even those semesters that he completed were curiously erratic in subject matter and grades. The only classes he appears to have attended with any consistency at the university were in French, mathematics, and English composition. It is unclear how much engineering instruction he received as formal education. The most relevant and useful training he received in his college "years" was in Conover's office. His knowledge seems to have come largely from experience and associates; he mastered what they knew and moved on.

But if he was a negligent and negligible student at the university, he took off socially and sartorially in the time he was there. For a young man who claimed to be both inexperienced and shy, he was quick to join a fraternity and he appears to have participated more actively in fraternity life than in the academic community. He managed to find the means for dues and entertainment and to dress the part, selling some of his father's books and relying, as usual, on his mother's generosity. He borrowed whenever and whatever he could, and he pawned his mother's Swiss gold watch, apparently with her consent. But his assumption of the outsider role was not all prideful; he was aware of being painfully poor at the same time that he was attracted to the pleasures of the privileged world of the university, and he was very concerned with cutting what Meryle Secrest has called, in her detailed biography and in the Italian fashion of stylish self-presentation, a *bella figura*. To that end, his mother sacrificed one of her most cherished possessions: a mink collar, which she sewed to his overcoat.

The *figura* he cut for the rest of his life was as important to his image as the history he invented; he dressed in the nineteenth-century manner of the artist as aesthete and dandy, and he played it to the hilt. Although today's artists have dropped romantic apparel for the international youth uniform of jeans and T-shirts, preferably paint-spattered, architects continue to dress in a way to set them apart from the rest of the world — a fashion statement that matters as much as one about art. The sartorial journey has been from flowing tie, to bow tie, to no tie, to hip, trendy all-black, with the occasional personal statement of a distinctive scarf or hat. Wright progressed from his mother's makeovers to custom tailoring; eventually, he set his own style, beyond fashion, in a cape and beret or brimmed porkpie hat, wielding an imperious cane as much for effect as for assistance, using it as pointer and weapon and coda to all of his critical remarks.

Inevitably, Madison became too small for his ambitions. He would want, and need, to go to Chicago, a city in the midst of a construction boom of epic dimensions in the 1880s. Chicago beckoned to any Middle Westerner hoping for an architectural career. For Wright, this was a natural, predestined move — Chicago offered prestigious buildings, important commissions, and a well-established architectural community. Its many new projects were attracting an astounding array of talented designers and audacious entrepreneurs. Determined to find a way to get there, Wright asked his malleable, but in this case, less than willing mother — visions of losing her son must have danced in her head — to write to one of the Uncles, Jenkin Lloyd Jones, a distinguished Unitarian preacher who was in the process of building a new church for his affluent Chicago congregation. He would find work in an architect's office, Wright told her, to help support her and his sisters, while fulfilling their mutual dream for his future. He used all his powers of persuasion, and the letter was finally sent.

"On no account," the preacher thundered back, undoubtedly to Anna's relief, "let the young man come to Chicago!" If he did, Uncle Jenkin warned, he would waste himself on fine clothes and girls; it was more important for him to complete his education in Madison. Wright took this as an insult and a signal to depart, since he was determined to do so anyway. He proceeded secretly, selling his father's copies of Plutarch's *Lives* and Gibbon's *Decline and Fall of the Roman Empire*, and his mother's mink collar, removed from his overcoat. After he had purchased a train ticket to Chicago, seven dollars were left for food and lodging until he found work. With a profound, if premature sense of destiny, he departed for "the Eternal City of the West."

What he found was far from eternal, and nothing like Rome. Chicago was being rebuilt after the fire, on a far more ambitious plan than its previous incarnations. According to Chicago historian Donald L. Miller, this was not the initial rebuilding that followed the great fire of 1871; that instant reconstruction was carried out as quickly as possible by builders working on the old models. It was a missed opportunity; in their anxiety to replace the old city, they "took even less thought the second time than they had on the first," Miller tells us. This "new" Chicago was outmoded almost as it appeared. The recession of 1873 brought work to a standstill until the end of the decade, and it wasn't until the economic revival of the 1880s that a second, transformational rebuilding began. In this reborn-again city, much was torn down and built anew for an expanding economy that required massive amounts of commercial space.

Chicago would be a different city this time. Architects and engineers were experimenting with new materials and structural systems that would become the basis of one of the most radical innovations in the history of building — the steel-skeleton-framed, curtain-walled skyscraper. Undisturbed by the lack of an architectural tradition, bound to no established style or previous pattern of construction, developers and their architects were able to design freely and innovatively. Unprecedented in size, these buildings served an energetic, flamboyant, risk-taking society with an aggressive commercial agenda. A flamboyant risk-taker himself, Wright would fit right in, and he would display that characteristic, personally and professionally, for the rest of his life.

The early Chicago high-rise may seem solidly handsome but somewhat earth-bound to our eyes today; at the time, and in the words of its most gifted designer, Louis Sullivan — soon to become Wright's employer — it was a "proud and soaring thing." With new materials, innovative structural systems, improved elevators, and advances in fireproofing, the Chicago model was revolutionary in concept, execution, and impact. Its practical virtues for the investor were the maximum use of costly land for the greatest return on the property, achieved by being able to build higher, with more accessible, rentable floors; the challenge for the architect was to find a new scale and style for an unprecedented building type. This was the start of a race for height and symbolism that has never stopped. What was happening in commercial centers like Chicago and New York changed cities everywhere, forever.

Optimism and ambition shared the air with the racket of cable cars and horse-drawn vehicles, the sights and sounds of construction, and the steam and smoke of industry in a city of enormous productive energy. Anything seemed possible, and each achievement built on the last. According to Miller, the average age of Chicago's architects was just under thirty at the beginning of the boom. "By 1886," he concludes, "Chicago — a place almost without architecture in 1880 — was the world center of architectural experimentation." Great firms, Burnham and Root, Adler and Sullivan, Holabird and Roche, were engaged on great projects — office buildings, trade headquarters and mercantile exchanges, theaters, department stores, and the mansions of the new millionaires. The Loop rivaled the stockyards as a center of awe and attention. An exceptional confluence of prosperity and civic and cultural leadership was building a city with a style and an image of its own.

According to the *Autobiography*, Wright arrived in Chicago at six o'clock on a rainy spring evening in 1887, dazzled by the electric lights he had never seen before, moving with the crowds in the dark and the wet, carried onto the opening bridge over the Chicago River, marveling at the dark water and the busy river scene below, joining the endless stream of people until hunger compelled him to stop. He spent seventy cents — a full 10 percent of his reserves — on something to eat, then drifted along until he reached the Chicago Opera House. He paid a dollar to go inside where it was dry and warm and to watch the musical "extravaganza," which he judged, in his one area of sophistication, the music learned from his father, to be florid and sentimental. Afterward, riding the cable car back and forth in a kind of tireless delirium, he was mesmerized by the billboards and glaring shopfront signs, overwhelmed by the traffic and noise and the impersonal masses of humanity. Finally, in a rooming house on a street chosen as much by chance as the rest of the evening's route, he fell into bed.

From there he set forth the next morning with a list made up from city directories or names he had heard in Allan Conover's office. He noted the feel of the three silver dollars and a dime left in his pocket. He tells the story in the *Autobiography*, playing down or omitting any fear or uncertainty that might undermine the bravado of the unknown, gifted young man seeking his fortune among strangers in the big city, although one suspects that the exhilaration and the possibilities kept him going. In the life he constructed for himself, vanity and verities merge.

And so we have two stories again. He claims to have come to Chicago without prospects or connections, vowing not to contact Uncle Jenkin, determined to succeed on his own. The first day proved fruitless. He made the rounds of architects' offices, their names now part of skyscraper history: S. S. Beman, the redoubtable engineer William Le Baron Jenney. He was rejected everywhere, even as he glimpsed drafting rooms bursting with activity. As he walked the streets in the fashionably narrow, uncomfortable "toothpick" shoes of his college wardrobe, he critically observed the city's famous buildings through the pain of his pinched feet — the Palmer House was "like an ugly old man whose wrinkles were all in the wrong place"; W. W. Boyington's Chicago Board of Trade, a "thin-chested, hard-faced, chamfered monstrosity," made him decide against seeking employment in that office. Sometimes he was seen by a kindly partner, more often by a dismissive draftsman. Returning to his inexpensive room for the night, he asked for something cheaper; a sympathetic desk clerk gave him one for seventy-five cents. He paid twenty cents for supper at a bakery. The next day, he visited five more offices, with the same results, and bought ten cents' worth of bananas for food. The fourth day, he tried three more offices, with no better luck.

His last stop was the firm of Joseph Lyman Silsbee, one of the most respected and fashionable architects of the time, who, not coincidentally, was building Uncle Jenkin's All Souls Church. Wright professes that he went anonymously, never revealing his connection or identity. A certain skepticism can be entertained at this disingenuous disclaimer. In 1886 — just the year before — Silsbee had built a replacement church for the Lloyd Joneses' family chapel in Spring Green, while Wright was still a student in Madison. He had actually participated in the work, checking interior construction details, and he had made a drawing of the Silsbee design, which was published, with the signature F. L. Wright, del. (delineator). An account of the chapel's construction in a Unitarian magazine mentioned that "a boy architect belonging to the family" had "looked after" things.

It seems unlikely that he left Madison without weighing the value of this connection. He must have gone to Chicago with some confidence that he could get a hearing, and even a job, in Silsbee's office, if all else failed, but he preferred to deny any such intent. He always maintained that Silsbee did not recognize him when he was called out to see his drawings by the draftsman who interviewed him. Wright claimed that he deliberately did not enlighten him. With or without recognition, Wright's drawing skills were already impressive; he drew almost as well as Silsbee, who was known for his seductive sketches of picturesque shingled houses with turrets, bay windows, porches, great hearths, and inglenooks, all in the popular Queen Anne style preferred by a prosperous middle class. It was only Silsbee's instant appreciation of the young man's superior talent, Wright informs us, that made him hire the aspiring young architect as a "tracer" at a salary of eight dollars a week. Wright had found his first job, with one of Chicago's most prestigious firms.

Well, maybe it happened that way. But does it really matter? A career, and a legend, were launched. And a friend was made — like Wright, the draftsman who interviewed him, Cecil Corwin, was a preacher's son, as was Silsbee himself. There was an instant rapport between the two young men of similar background, who shared a love of music, literature, and the theater. Sensing that young Wright was hungry, Corwin took him to a restaurant famous for its corned beef hash, which Wright always remembered as the best he ever ate. Then Corwin took him home. He was happy and grateful to be shown to the Corwins' guest room; Cecil's father was recently widowed, and his sister took care of the two men. Sensing Wright's concern about the family he had left behind — four days had passed and he knew his mother's anxiety must be reaching epic proportions — Corwin brought a pen and writing paper to the room. Wright then asked if he could borrow ten dollars, which he would pay back out of his salary. He relates this incident in the *Autobiography* in his usual disarming way, confessing that borrowing was a practice he would become shamelessly addicted to. Corwin quietly left the money, and Wright enclosed it in the letter to his mother with the triumphant news of his new job and life.

When he reported for work the next morning, he found the drawing boards filled with Queen Anne houses; he would learn a great deal about domestic architecture in Silsbee's employ. But he would soon begin to think of Silsbee's facile sketches as "pretty pictures" and develop ideas of his own. Of particular interest to him were the designs for Uncle Jenkin's church. A trip to the construction site with Cecil Corwin resulted in what could not have been a totally unanticipated meeting

— Uncle Jenkin was found supervising progress, and a reunion with the wayward nephew took place. Nor would this have been an unwelcome event; the advantages of being part of the distinguished preacher's family with entrée into some of Chicago's best social and professional circles could not have escaped the ambitious young man. He had to be aware of how helpful this fortuitous encounter would be.

Although he was invited to remain at the Corwins, he soon moved to a furnished room on the strength of a four-dollar raise, which was immediately eaten up by the additional expense. Never one to suffer in silence, and always convinced that he was worth considerably more than he was being given, he asked for a raise to fifteen dollars, and when it was refused, he left Silsbee to go to another firm, Beers, Clay and Dutton. A cycle of self-advancing moves provided increases in salary and a range of learning experiences, which Wright was quick to take advantage of, or to abandon when their usefulness ended. He pursued his course directly and astutely. Nor was any embarrassment involved. When he felt that the creative level of Beers, Clay and Dutton was too low, he informed the partners that there was no senior designer from whom he could learn, and unashamedly went back to Silsbee, who rehired him at eighteen dollars.

Anna wrote once a week, reminding him about Goodness and Truth, proper diet, warm underwear, and appropriate companions. He was not to worry about her. She had sold what was left of his father's library and received a few hundred dollars from her brothers from the sale of their father's farm, and she would sell the Madison house and come to Chicago when he needed her. "Always very brave she was," Wright wrote in the *Autobiography*, "but I knew what she wanted — she wanted to come down to live with me." Anna was not about to be left behind. And her son knew his duty. Now that he was earning eighteen dollars, he would bring Anna and his little sister, Maginel, to Chicago; his other sister, Jane, was already teaching somewhere in the country. This was the time to make the move.

He favored the lakefront, but Anna found it cold, and she did not like the crowds and raffishness of the city. After a search of surrounding suburbs, Oak Park, just west of Chicago, was chosen for its wide, tree-lined streets; it reminded her of Madison and its unassailable respectability was attested to by the name "Saints' Rest," which had been given to it for its many churches. Anna knew Oak Park's Universalist pastor, a Miss Augusta Chapin, a formidable woman in rustling black taffeta and a large gold cross, who owned a proper redbrick house on Forest Avenue. A deal was soon struck that would allow them to share Miss Chapin's home until more permanent arrangements could be made.

In less than a year, Wright had consolidated his position as a draftsman in one of Chicago's best offices and published a drawing of another of Silsbee's chapels, this time signed Frank L. Wright, Archt. (architect, a big step up from the del., or draftsman, signature of the earlier Silsbee chapel drawing), and he had designed and constructed his first building on his own, the Hillside Home School in Spring Green, for his Aunts Nell and Jane, in 1887. Silsbee had apparently allowed him to take the necessary time to execute the commission.

But Wright soon realized that he had omitted the firm of Adler and Sullivan from his calculations, and he knew now that this was the most important office in Chicago for the kind of creative work he admired. Silsbee represented the top of the establishment; Adler and Sullivan were on architecture's leading edge. He wondered, briefly, how the firm could have escaped his notice originally; it had much more to offer him. The partners were a strangely matched but compatible pair — Dankmar Adler, a solid, amiable, dependable businessman and expert structural engineer, a member of Chicago's large German-Jewish establishment, and Louis H. Sullivan, a handsome, reclusive Irishman trained at the Massachusetts Institute of Technology and the Ecole des Beaux-Arts in Paris, whose brilliant work was defining the new tall building. The two men collaborated closely in every area of the practice.

Construction had begun in early 1887 on the firm's most ambitious project, the Auditorium Building, at Congress Parkway and Michigan Avenue, a structure that was to combine a large office block and tower, a luxury hotel, and an elaborate new auditorium for opera, concerts, and theater. Wright was spoiling for a project of this size and distinction, and lost no time pursuing the opportunity to be part of it. There are, not surprisingly, several versions of how he got himself hired. His own story is that word came to him through another draftsman that the Adler and Sullivan office was virtually begging him to apply. It is more likely that he heard the rumor that Sullivan needed assistants to help him handle the Auditorium work and quickly determined that this was his next move.

Wright left Silsbee, not without feelings of guilt, since the older architect had been good to him; Silsbee expressed mild annoyance and genuine regret when confronted with his young draftsman's departure. But guilt was assuaged by rationalization, a process in which Wright was becoming expert, indulging in the kind of reasoning that fogged questionable or self-interested behavior with higher moral issues. Did not growth always require and inflict pain? Wright asked rhetorically in the *Autobiography*. Wasn't the pursuit and achievement of excellence the product of discomfort or anguish, was not life, in fact, accompanied by a sequence of such painful episodes leading to the fulfillment of one's highest capabilities? "Does not every forward movement have its own pang?" he rationalized, with appropriate rhetorical passion. And shouldn't it be understood that this was a natural process, he concluded, his rhetoric and reason taking flight, as natural as the tree that lets go of the top leaves that shadow its lower branches so they can develop fully, or of the perennials that rise to bloom through the winter's dead growth?

And wasn't Silsbee at fault, too, he asked Cecil, pushing the argument to even higher and more questionable ground, for not aspiring to the best he had in him, for settling for those "pretty pictures"; wasn't his architecture a defection, a lie? Wasn't it wrong, didn't it make him less admirable as a man and model? Shouldn't it be absolutely essential, in the deepest biblical sense of Right, and Truth, he insisted, not to betray one's duty to aspire to the best one could achieve? There are complex layers here of ego and opportunism, honest soul-searching and self-serving self-exoneration. The pursuit of an artistic ideal is often inseparable from driving ambition; one fuels the other, and both center on the realization of self, no matter how the process is disguised as disinterested philosophical inquiry. The convoluted arguments about right and wrong were those of a preacher, and as his son Lloyd would remark in later years, Wright came from a family of preachers: he had the soul of a preacher and used the language of a preacher. He was given to delivering sermons. His writing and speeches were always homilies on architecture, with terrible scoldings for the unconverted.

He was like every other artist committed to a vision — no obstacle, no scruple, must stand in the way. Because no red carpet is ever rolled out for ideas that shake beliefs, disturb precedent, and threaten the comfortably familiar, every gifted innovator has fought, fair and foul, to make others see and value the work and ideas that set great art apart from the acceptable and the accessible. Both the producer and the product are rejected. It is a very hard sell. Wright called architecture the "mother of the arts" for its embrace of reality and its power to elevate the human condition in both practical and poetic terms. For the artist, the dream is destiny. Making impossible promises and employing seductive charm is permissible to get the dream built. If it requires scheming, wheedling, and bold-faced lying, the ends justify the means. It helps if your banner is "truth against the world."

4

The groundwork, real and rationalized, was set for his rapid rise. Wright was hired immediately by Adler and Sullivan at the salary he requested, twenty-five dollars, although in his usual fashion he thought he could have asked for forty and gotten it. Sullivan apparently recognized the young man's exceptional talents as a draftsman but, even more important, the two bonded; biographer Brendan Gill has called it an immediate "infatuation," suggesting an unacknowledged homoerotic element. Whatever chemistry may have existed between them, consciously or subconsciously — without indulging in questionable psychobiography — there was undoubtedly a quick recognition of shared interests and attitudes focused on their intense preoccupation with the art of building. There was surely mutual admiration, and mutual need, but the speculative search for hidden sexual meaning is an unnecessary stretch of a natural attachment between the two, beyond the professional closeness, clearly nurtured by Wright, that soon made him, in his own words, "the pencil in the master's hand."

Sullivan, darkly handsome, moody and aloof, spoke to no one; he would stride through the drafting room without greeting its occupants or even acknowledging their presence, but he would stay after hours and talk long and passionately into the night with his young assistant about the subjects that absorbed them both. He found a sympathetic companion in the talented young man who was so eager to listen and learn, and to whom he could expound, not only on architecture, but also on the music of Wagner, the poetry of Whitman, the philosophy of Herbert Spencer, or any other subject that interested him at the time. For Wright, Sullivan was the teacher and role model he had sought. Eager to absorb everything he could, he was also keenly aware that this association was the key to his future. It was to be a legendary relationship — Sullivan as the *lieber meister,* the beloved master — although the relationship was to end bitterly in a few years. What passed between them has been studied ever since; the only element that remains unquestioned is that this was a unique collision of genius, a collaboration and exchange of two extraordinary talents.

The phrase *lieber meister,* used repeatedly and reverently by Wright, was not unusual in the predominantly Germanic culture of Chicago. Nor was Wright alone in his devotion to Sullivan; there were other acolytes and admirers. But the intellectual and ideological bond between the two men was exceptional. Sullivan could command Wright's attention at all hours — there were nights when Wright went home late and to bed without supper, rising early the next morning to return to the office. Both believed devoutly in the need to create a new architecture to suit the changing conditions of contemporary American life, and each was determined, in his own way, to make it real. Whatever the source of the attraction between them, and however critics view the interplay of influence — revisionist historians see it flowing from the younger to the older man, as well as from master to pupil — the importance of Sullivan to Wright is beyond argument, as Wright himself never ceased to acknowledge.

Wright always gave the impression that Sullivan was a much older man, almost a father figure, although there was only about ten years' difference in their ages. Sullivan was in his thirties and at the top of his profession, and Wright was a beginner, not long off the farm. Sullivan had sampled Paris's cosmopolitan pleasures while he was at the Ecole des Beaux-Arts. He was a sophisticate, with experience in matters of life and art that the boy from Wisconsin sorely lacked and consciously craved. All this put a considerable distance between them.

Wright was an avid student, and soon became so skilled an assistant that he could create his own version of Sullivan's characteristic ornament, easily imitating the rich foliate curves of its interlaced Celtic forms. The way he could anticipate and carry out Sullivan's ideas was the architectural equivalent of finishing his sentences. Even at this early date, he was clear in his own mind about his preference for a cleaner, more geometric style; he rejected the picturesque pastiches that dominated the office's domestic practice. Sullivan had no interest in designing houses; those "courtesy" commissions for his clients were handed over to Wright, with his blessing. Wright produced about a half dozen of these houses for the firm between 1890 and 1892. Done on office overtime, for extra pay, they were a welcome addition to his income, which was never enough for those luxuries he considered necessities, the books and Japanese prints he began to collect. At least one of the commissions, a Chicago town house for James Charnley, built in 1891, was a surprisingly mature and masterly work. The elegant symmetry of its unadorned brick façade, broken only by a projecting balcony with restrained Renaissance details, was a significant departure from the elaborate eclecticism of Chicago's newly mansion-lined streets.

He could not have picked a better place or time to continue the engineering education that had started in Conover's office. Dankmar Adler was a highly respected, Army-trained engineer, and the firm attracted the large projects that required the most advanced construction techniques. And while Wright was never close with the other draftsmen, he liked and befriended Paul Mueller, an engineer who worked directly with Adler as his construction foreman. It was the beginning of a long association; Mueller became Wright's engineer on many of his buildings after he started independent practice, reinforcing Wright's innate and acquired engineering skills with his practical expertise.

Wright not only pushed the current limits of architecture, his ideas also tested the limits of engineering as it was practiced at the time. Because there were no precise rules or procedures for his designs, he relied as much on an empirical sense of structure as on formal calculations. He always told his clients that they were embarking on an experimental voyage. Few, if any, declined the risk. The dramatically projecting and hovering roofs, the houses hung from hillsides or suspended over streams, the towers supported like trees with taproot foundations and branching floors — all the bold departures of his future work — went beyond conventional practice.

When he was challenged, which happened frequently, he indulged his flair for high-risk showmanship, staging dramatic demonstrations to convince clients that his buildings were structurally sound. He ordered sandbags heaped on the top of one of the slender, tapering columns of the Johnson Wax Administration Building of 1936, far in excess of the actual load, in a theatrical display of its strength before it finally failed. A famous running battle over engineering took place during the construction of Fallingwater, built in 1935 for Pittsburgh department store owner Edgar Kaufmann. Extremely skeptical about Wright's structural expertise, Kaufmann called in his own engineers to review the house's radical cantilevered construction. They revised Wright's specifications, he threatened to resign, and then secretly did it his own way. Almost seventy years later, Fallingwater's cantilevers began to deflect dangerously, as materials aged and stresses took their toll. Restoration required solutions routinely practiced now that did not exist at the time.

There is a kind of collective *schadenfreude* in the revelation of defects in great buildings and flaws in great men; nothing is hailed as joyfully by press and public as the errors, imperfections, or miscalculations of those who have challenged the status quo by embracing the unfamiliar against the numbingly ordinary. There are building failures every day — bridges give way, roofs collapse, and ceilings fall — recorded routinely in engineering publications; yet they go unnoticed unless human tragedy is involved. But the failure of anything that has been elevated above normal human expectations and easy acceptance is received as divine retribution for artistic hubris.

Repairs and retrofitting are common in old buildings, and Wright's unorthodox solutions proved vulnerable. Flaws and failures — greeted with the special satisfaction that makes the hero or artist mortal, like the rest of us — have become an indispensable part of the Wright legend. The tales of leaks in Wright buildings, real and apocryphal, are legion. There are one-bucket, two-bucket, or three-bucket houses, with the number revised upward, as needed. Most of the stories are true, and many houses have been fixed with better flashing and silicones. To one client, who complained of water on his desk, Wright famously replied, "Move your desk." As another deployed pails and pans to catch the flow, his wife remarked, "Well, that's what you get for leaving a work of art out in the rain." If there was a price to be paid for departures from convention, Wright considered it negligible. So, evidently, did many of his clients. More likely, his confidence in his own infallibility was such that he didn't consider it at all. He never played it safe — in art or in life — and apology was not his style.

Wright's first experience of large-scale construction and engineering took place in the Adler and Sullivan office, working on the Auditorium Building, which would require four years to complete. As described by Donald Miller in his Chicago history, *City of the Century*, "200 men and 30 teams of horses were used to break the frozen ground in early 1887 for the great pit that would hold the largest private building in America. And it went forward with incredible speed, into the night with the aid of electric floodlights and through two hard Chicago winters."

The job required far more drawing than Sullivan could produce, and Wright was given responsibility for detailing many of his ideas. In this privileged position, he was seen as Sullivan's favorite; as Wright tells it, he was aware of the hostility to his rapid rise, and expecting trouble, began to take secret boxing lessons from a Colonel Monsterry, a name he carefully records. The colonel would have preferred foils as a more gentlemanly defense, but settled for improving Wright's knockout punches. What his tormentors could not have known from Wright's small size was how much strength and endurance he had developed from all the hauling and lifting and piling of "tired on tired" during those summers on the farm. After much verbal and other harassment, including having his hat thrown down the stairs, he claims to have retaliated by knocking the chief troublemaker off his stool, breaking his glasses — an unsportsmanlike sin in the rules of engagement of the time. In the free-for-all that followed, he suffered stab wounds in the neck from a drafting knife. The fight ended with a resounding wallop of Wright's T square, which knocked his chief assailant out. This triumph, presumably, was followed by a wary peace on both sides.

As his professional fortunes rose, his personal life was also improving rapidly. Upon completion of the Auditorium Building, the firm moved to the top of the tower, on the seventeenth floor. Wright had his own office, next to Sullivan's. His friendship with Cecil Corwin gave him a companion of his own age. He was "going to school to Cecil," as he put it, whose company provided not only pleasure, but also a chance to learn from a more worldly young man with the social skills that Wright hoped to acquire. He was still insecure and shy with girls — his mother had ensured his sexual innocence in the atmosphere of pious rectitude maintained by the Uncles and the Aunts. Neither alcohol nor smoking was permitted, and whatever

Wright's later transgressions, drinking was not one of them. He had good looks, youth, charm, and wit. His sense of style and passion for fine things was already highly developed and would dictate his future priorities and make for permanent, profligate indebtedness. In Cecil's company, he was gaining ease and assurance, discovering the joys and entertainments of the city.

He had gone to Chicago with valuable connections, although they were always denied, and he undoubtedly knew that the quickest and smoothest road to social success would be through Uncle Jenkin's church. In her weekly letters before her move to Oak Park, Anna urged him to stay close to his uncle, who had become an important figure in Chicago as the leader of a prominent Unitarian congregation. After Wright's "chance" meeting with his uncle, he was immediately received into the family circle and introduced to the distinguished acquaintances of his uncle's world. These were the associations that he needed, the people who became his clients and friends, and he would have been naïve indeed not to have understood this, or taken advantage of the opportunities. He had already demonstrated a native, calculated shrewdness in the ambitious pursuit of his career. Now the aspiring architect was exposed to a wide range of prominent religious and literary figures. Among those liberal and intellectual leaders and reformers who came regularly to the Lloyd Jones house was the social reformer Jane Addams; Wright would give a talk on "The Art and Craft of the Machine" at Hull House in 1901. He began to enjoy the company of the successful young members of the Chicago business establishment. The church, which operated as a social center and a religious institution, offered an extraordinary array of activities and opportunities.

It was at a costume party following an amateur theatrical production that he met Catherine Lee Tobin, the attractive young daughter of one of Uncle Jenkin's wealthy parishioners. Wright described her as tall and slender, with fair skin, blue eyes, rosy cheeks, and a mass of red curls. She walked with a "kind of light-hearted gaiety" right into his heart. Only sixteen, and still in high school, she was apparently as smitten with him as he was with her. It would have been a youthful romance under normal circumstances, but after such long, zealous protection against the sins of the flesh, it was not surprising that he fell seriously in love with the first pretty girl who entered his life. The courtship that followed was watched with intense disapproval by the parents on both sides. When she reached seventeen they were determined to marry. Anna was firmly opposed, and Catherine's parents would have none of it. They were told that they were much too young, and one can easily imagine Catherine's family's objection to their beloved and indulged daughter's insistence on marrying a penniless young architect, as well as Anna's reluctance to so quickly lose her son. Catherine was sent to visit a relative at Mackinac Island for three months as a cure, a banishment the two young people saw as a romantic obstacle that had absolutely no effect on their plans. The wedding took place on June 1, 1889, when the bride was not quite eighteen. It was a rainy day, and Anna and the in-laws wept copiously. Just one week from his twenty-second birthday, an accomplished, but still apprentice architect, Wright was now a married man.

He had already informed Sullivan that he intended to marry, being careful to add that he could afford neither a wife nor the home they would need on the money he earned. Sullivan, unwilling to lose "the good pencil in his hand," rose to the occasion and offered him a five-year contract and a loan for the house. Sullivan himself inspected and approved the lot Wright selected in Oak Park, a rustic corner plot on Forest and Chicago avenues. Fortuitously, it included an existing cottage for Anna. Wise enough to know that she could not control him and determined to remain part of his life, she settled for proximity. After the land was purchased, $3,500 was left for construction, a sum Wright promptly exceeded by $1,200, a fact he never mentioned to Sullivan; the cost overrun established another lifelong practice.

The newlyweds moved into their home that same year. It was a small house, with a high, pitched roof sheltering two projecting bays accommodating a large window as well as an offset entrance. An entry area and living room were dominated by an arched brick fireplace and inglenook. A dining room and kitchen completed the ground floor, with bedrooms above. Under the eaves was an upstairs drafting room.

Children and creditors came rapidly and together. Four boys and two girls would arrive in quick succession, a number that shocked the young couple's more abstemious, or careful, neighbors. As the home filled with the beautiful things that Wright seemed to require like meat and drink, the provisioners of those basic necessities were left unpaid; money for a grocer's bill for several hundred dollars — an unheard-of sum at that time — had to be borrowed, adding to a growing load of debt. When the house was not in a domestic uproar, it was being torn apart and reassembled by Wright, who spent much time rearranging furniture and accessories. His homes were always being altered or added to, as his needs and his vision changed. A photograph of the extended family, which included his wife and his son Lloyd, his sisters, Jane and Maginel, and his mother, set up and taken by Wright — he was an avid and talented photographer — shows the group seated in front of the house on a Persian carpet he had dragged out and draped across the steps to create an appropriate aesthetic background.

Space became an urgent priority, and the upstairs drafting room was soon divided into two small bedrooms. In 1895 Wright added the Playroom, a handsome space topped by a barrel vault with a central skylight, the curving ribs traced in dark wood. Light flooded from the room's twenty-foot-high ceiling and through a continuous band of windows where the ceiling vault sprang from Roman brick walls. An oak floor was patterned in the circles and squares that had stayed with Wright from the memory of the childhood Froebel "gifts." In a lunette above a massive fireplace at the end of the room was an *Arabian Nights* mural, a painting commissioned by Wright; festive clusters of hanging glass globes formed chandeliers, completing the fairy tale atmosphere. A balcony invited amateur theatricals, which were soon supplied. The Playroom was an artful, enchanted space, conceived with Wright's already accustomed ease and theatricality.

In a memoir written in 1946, *My Father Who Is on Earth*, Wright's son John, who also became an architect, has recorded a bittersweet mix of love, admiration, guilty resentment, and aching self-doubt as he came to terms with a difficult and demanding father, as both parent and occasional collaborator. A rare and revealing portrait of Wright's oldest son, Lloyd, who studied landscape architecture and moved to California, is provided by Thomas S. Hines. Lloyd pushed his natural inheritance to a bold expressionistic style in a series of remarkable California houses built from the 1930s to the 1950s. He also spent time working with his father and had an equally troubling relationship. But he paints a poignant picture of the Oak Park house, describing a special childhood spent in a special place.

"Double-leveled rooms of one and two stories; scattered vases filled with leaves and wild flowers, massive fireplaces. . . . A Persian lantern, samovars, windows which met and turned the corners, light filtering through fret-sawed ceiling grilles, sunshine and shadows . . . a piano . . . a life-size bronze bust of Beethoven, an old carved Chinese chair . . . books . . . colored, patterned, and textured papers in large folios, piled up and pushed on wide ledges on either side of a long window" — the disarming disarray of the artist and collector, an ambience at once progressive and reminiscent of the Victorian aesthete.

He never forgot his impressions of the Playroom. He writes of his sensation of the burst of light as he entered it, after coming through the "narrow, long, low-arched, dimly-lit passageway that led to it," and the magic of the flickering firelight that brought the fairy-tale characters to life, the floor "strewn with queer dolls, building blocks, funny mechanical toys, animals that moved about and wagged their strange heads." The Playroom was the precursor of a pattern of contrast and surprise that was central to all of Wright's work — the small, shadowed, restricted entry that opens to the revelation of a great room, the controlled sequence of light and space.

But Lloyd also remembered, with the hindsight of maturity, that this wonderful place of his childhood was "a continuously mortgaged and periodically remodeled experimental laboratory of design and finance," as were all of Wright's homes — tenuously and riskily paid for, extravagantly and beautifully furnished with Japanese screens, Chinese porcelains and bronzes, Indian statuary, oriental carpets, and exotic artifacts from distant times and places. The remarkable rationalization Wright offered for this cavalier attitude toward financial obligations was that none of his children should grow up without the experience of beauty. There was no contest between solvency and his aesthetic priorities and habitual self-indulgence. The enrichment of eye and mind mattered more to him than a reputation for fiscal probity. He was as willfully helpless against the acquisitive urge as a compulsive gambler who cannot resist playing the odds — he sometimes spent all he earned on the things he often declared he could not live without.

There is a famous tale — this one true — that documents his casual financial habits and personal priorities. Finding himself without funds for the return to Oak Park from Chicago one day, he went to the office of his cousin Richard Lloyd Jones — who would become a prominent Midwestern publisher and the client for one of Wright's great houses — to borrow the price of a train ticket. He took the money and returned shortly with some irresistible Japanese prints he had purchased on the way to the station, still in need of the loan to get home.

Lloyd never questioned that the Oak Park house was the source of his own sense of beauty and love of art. But the backgrounds that architects create for themselves are more than homes. They are a discreet form of self-advertisement, the way they present themselves and their design credos and credentials to the world. There were frequent parties in the Playroom; the Wright-designed setting, toys and all, served as much to impress a growing circle of friends and clients as to accommodate the children's games. In later years, Lloyd would rescue objects he remembered and loved, sometimes finding them in the ruins of a Taliesin fire, arguing with his father over their possession in a way that had as much to do with his emotionally complex childhood as with their beauty or value.

Wright's presence and standing in the community were noticeably on the rise. He was probably the highest paid draftsman in any Chicago firm, supervising a staff of thirty in the Adler and Sullivan office. But as the financial burdens of the exploding family and his expensive lifestyle became more pressing, he was caught in a nonstop financial shell game of loans and deferrals. He became known in Oak Park as much for his unpaid accounts as for his flair for elegant living. Bills were pushed into some deep, dark hole until creditors or the bank served notice and a bit of last-minute legerdemain preserved the status quo. He kept a fine horse, on which he became a familiar figure as he rode around Oak Park in well-cut tweeds; later, when automobiles were available, he was never without a handsome fast car. He cut a conspicuously fashionable and sometimes eccentric figure in custom-tailored suits and costumes of his own design ordered from a Mr. Hutchinson in Chicago, Sullivan's tailor.

Wright stayed with Adler and Sullivan until 1893, working in the Chicago office by day and in the Oak Park house at night. To meet expenses, which meant, for Wright, not just supporting a family but sustaining a standard of living that included season tickets to the Chicago Orchestra, he began to design "bootleg" houses, as he termed them, on his own time. But there was a significant difference between this secret activity and the houses he had carried out for the firm on office overtime with Sullivan's knowledge and consent. Wright's five-year contract specifically prohibited moonlighting, and the bootleg houses were sure to come to Sullivan's attention. When he found out, he was furious; he fired Wright immediately. In his anger, Sullivan refused to surrender the deed to Wright's property, which he had held as collateral for the loan, although the money had been repaid. The document was eventually returned through the intervention of Sullivan's more conciliatory elder partner, Dankmar Adler. The break was bitter and lasting; the two men did not speak again for seventeen years.

It is impossible to know what factors

may have contributed to Sullivan's extraordinary response; he was soon to go into a tragic downward spiral of depression and inactivity. But there was certainly a sense of betrayal of trust and friendship — although he had never called Wright by anything except his last name — that went far deeper than the breaking of a contract. It was a critically difficult moment in Sullivan's career; his architectural preeminence had plummeted with the opening of the World's Columbian Exposition in Chicago in 1893, where the dreamlike Great White City designed by East Coast architects in the classical manner was wildly popular. Sullivan's own Transportation Building, a striking structure of polychromed concentric arches in russet and gold, rich with his interlaced ornament, was seen as hopelessly out of step with the snowy grandeur of the fair's paint-and-plaster Renaissance palaces. Clients abandoned him for the newly fashionable academic classicism of Daniel Burnham, McKim, Mead and White, Richard Morris Hunt, and the members of a social and professional old-boy network to which the outsider, the moody and brilliant Irishman, never belonged.

In Sullivan's anguished assessment, the

fair set the course of architecture back fifty years. The optimism and high purpose of the American ideal of progress that he and Wright believed would be expressed in new ways of designing and building gave way to the established forms of a traditional Eurocentric architectural culture well into the twentieth century. A depression the same year as the world's fair cut back commissions that might have been Sullivan's; his jobs declined in number and he was without work after 1910. Emotional, introspective, bitterly resentful, and unable to come to terms with the reversal of fortune or his own temperament, he was to spend his final years living in poverty, fighting a hopeless vendetta with fate, exacerbated by his obsessive concern with the cruel and bizarre turn in architectural taste.

Wright, as usual, rationalized his behavior in designing the bootleg houses with his own interpretation of his contractual obligations. Whatever rupture took place in his personal or professional relationships he reasoned away as morally defensible or excused by inevitable circumstances that left him no other course of action. His needs were urgent, a society that condemned him held false standards, his personal values put him beyond censure in his own mind. It was Wright who finally made the overture to Sullivan, by then destitute, ill, and alone. Between 1910 and 1924, when Sullivan died, he gave his *lieber meister* small sums of money, and the proud and desperate letters he received from Sullivan are heart wrenching. The man who represented the most creative tendencies of an innovative American architecture never saw the realization of his dream that the twentieth century would bring.

When Wright left Adler and Sullivan in 1893, he opened an office in the Schiller Building, one of the firm's earlier designs. He shared it for a while with his friend Cecil Corwin, but it was used primarily as a place to meet his Chicago clients. He continued to work at home, as he had for both the overtime and the bootleg jobs. The houses that had caused the rupture were a curious, transitional lot, hybrids of his own ideas and of the currently popular styles that his clients must have requested and which Wright was not yet well enough established to refuse. The lordly take-it-or-leave-it autocrat was yet to come. There were some colonial and Tudor revivals, and a few odd, top-heavy experiments with arcaded, Florentine-style loggias that were soon abandoned. What they shared was a consistent simplification of academic detail and a superior sense of scale. Traditional cornices were replaced by overhanging eaves, gabled roofs gave way to the hip roofs he favored, and interior walls shifted and disappeared.

Once Wright was on his own, his work quickly flowered into the tradition-shattering and history-making houses of his Prairie style, accompanied by a philosophy of "organic architecture," which he proclaimed, and preached, for the rest of his life. The name "Prairie houses" has been alternately praised and derided — accepted as a revolutionary concept of regional domestic architecture, or attacked as a pretentious misnomer for houses far from the prairie on suburban Chicago lots. The reference appeared in print in 1901, when a model home Wright designed for Edward Bok, the head of the Curtis Publishing Company, was published in *Ladies' Home Journal* as "A Home in a Prairie Town." Bok was an advocate of better house design; he had asked a number of prominent architects to contribute progressive house concepts to the magazine and they had all refused. Wright understood immediately that this would bring his work to an audience beyond the Middle West, and would also give him an opportunity to display his ideas untainted by client compromise.

Two of his designs were published in the same year. The houses could be built on a budget of $7,000 and $5,800, respectively, and the plans could be purchased from the magazine. There was no rush to buy the plans, but the type was clearly established: a low, horizontal structure, rather than a high, straight-sided box, with a relationship to the land that the rigidly vertical dwelling had never acknowledged. Continuous bands of casement windows ran under low, hovering roofs; the conventional formal parlor was replaced by a living room, dining room, and study that flowed together in a hearth-centered, single space. Interior walls were suppressed or minimized to emphasize openness. The focus of the house was the large, central fireplace that suggested a family gathered together in its embracing warmth; a broad chimney appeared to secure the building to the earth, under a sheltering roof. The houses continue to be intensely appealing.

In Wright's own mind, the westward sweep from Chicago to the prairie towns that still existed close by at the turn of the last century was easily rationalized and romanticized as a basis for his designs. Once established, the type appeared wherever the client had land, from a suburban street to a wooded lot. Wright's love of the gently undulating hills and open vistas of his Wisconsin childhood led naturally to his belief that the house should be part of the land in a figurative or metaphorical sense. Most architects give their creations some kind of rationale based on a sensed or expressed inner belief or conviction, often stretched beyond easy credibility. But the long, low lines, interlocking forms, and open spatial planning of Wright's Prairie houses not only "broke the box," as he put it, of the traditional house with its unyielding vertical plan and circulation, they created a connection with the site that broke the barrier between indoors and out with banks of windows, terraces, and indirect approaches through visually related landscaped settings. Even when the house did not escape the restricted suburban lot, it made it into a different kind of place.

Where did this house come from? The most assiduous search of the literature turns up nothing like it being built at the time. There are no obvious precursors, no published look-alikes, no neat icono-graphical clues to a developing style. The fiction that Wright insisted on throughout his life, the myth that he maintained, was that his work was pure invention, a kind of architectural virgin birth, that the concepts sprang fully formed from his own mind without debt or precedent. In one sense this was so; he was an "original," as he claimed, a maverick, the inventor of some-thing new. But the truth is more rewarding; if one digs deeper, it becomes clear that what seems so spontaneously created actu-ally drew on many interests and influences, synthesizing them in a way that was both revolutionary and beautiful, and uniquely his own.

Wright was a magpie — a keenly intelli-gent, insatiable collector of everything that appealed to him from an infinite variety of sources. He was a cultivated man from a family that held knowledge in the highest esteem; his heritage encouraged openness to ideas. Tireless in his pursuit of all that intrigued him, an omnivorous reader and keen observer, he was attracted to the most progressive and eclectic tastes and ideas of the nineteenth century. Like all architects, he was well aware of other talented practi-tioners who broke new ground and whose buildings he admired; he studied them with care. He knew exactly what was worthy of attention in the work of the establishment architects he professed to scorn; while he rejected Silsbee's fussy Queen Anne houses and spurned McKim, Mead and White's Beaux Arts monuments, he was clearly receptive to the simpler, less formal, natural-wood "shingle style" both firms employed for country homes.

He remembered everything, but copied nothing, absorbing what he liked and learned into his own creative thinking. Anthony Alofsin, a particularly perceptive chronicler of his work, has defined the process succinctly: "Wright's genius lay in his powers to assimilate, abstract and to emulate without ever resorting to imitation." His brilliance lies not only in the uniqueness of his vision, but in the way it connects with the most creative currents of his own time, while transforming those sources into a personal expression that changed the course of the building art.

He would, of course, deny any indebtedness forever. He insisted that he owed nothing to anyone, that the rest of the profession consisted of knaves and fools at worst, or merely the unenlightened. He alone represented architectural truth — the rest owed everything to him. He declared himself the enemy of the Academy and the Western classical tradition. But the fact is that he both stood apart from his times and was a product of his times — another paradox of his art and life. Wright was an active participant in the intellectual ferment and creative inquiry that prefigured modernism in the arts. What he carefully denied was that he was in touch with every new development, every contemporary current, every innovation here and in Europe, through books, magazines, direct observation, and professional contacts abroad. Although he expressed admiration in the *Autobiography* for the work he saw in Vienna and Berlin, the only influences he ever publicly acknowledged were the art of Japan and the philosophy of Viollet-le-Duc — the first because it offered lessons in the intrinsic qualities of materials and the elimination of the nonessential, the second because it taught a moral aesthetic of structure. Both could be quoted without compromising his creative independence.

The dark wood trim and light stucco walls of his early houses reflect his fascination with the Japanese architecture he saw for the first time in the Ho-o-den at the

1893 Chicago world's fair. Intrigued by the building's simplicity, elegant craft, and structural lightness, he praised it as "natural," "organic," and "modern." His first trip abroad was not the traditional European grand tour, but a trip to Tokyo in 1905, where he left his wife and companions to make long detours alone to the provinces in curious "native" clothing of his own devising, immersing himself in Japanese art and culture, returning with his first exotic purchases.

It is not hard to discover, from his books and correspondence, that he was an admirer of the new art and craft of the Vienna Secession. His initial encounter with a Secession building was Josef Maria Olbrich's Austrian Pavilion at the 1904 St. Louis Louisiana Purchase Exposition; he returned repeatedly to analyze its unusual design. He had contacts with English and Dutch modernist pioneers, some of whom expressed great interest in his early buildings and came to Chicago to see them. The Germans and the Dutch were the first to recognize Wright's work, in major publications.

With the recession over, his commissions soared, and so did his confidence. By 1904, he had completed at least a dozen

Prairie houses. Considered strange interlopers by their neighbors, they are classics today. There were three versions: a basic, standardized type that Wright felt was accessible to people of modest means, a moderate model with better materials and more special features for those who could pay for them, and an expensive, custom form, exquisitely and dictatorially designed, down to the last handcrafted detail.

His clients were successful, well-educated, upper-middle-class businessmen, leaders in the community, political "progressives" with liberal leanings and cultural interests, who could afford the cost of a substantial home. Wright's work, representing an advanced, "enlightened" view of architecture, intrigued them; it also appealed to their aesthetically and intellectually involved wives. Like so many patrons of the arts, they became supporters of the new; their homes were brave gestures of informed patronage in what Wright habitually scorned as a surrounding sea of suburban bourgeois philistinism. They also became his friends and champions. Both would be needed in the years ahead, when success would turn into scandal, and scandal into tragedy of epic dimensions.

5

Wright was now employing draftsmen of his own and it became imperative to add more work space in Oak Park. The Playroom was followed quickly by the Studio, in 1895, along the Chicago Avenue side of the property. An open loggia reached by stairs behind a low wall brought the visitor from the street to an offset entrance; behind the loggia was a generous reception hall, with Wright's study just beyond. Immediately to the left was a large, double-height drafting room, the studio proper, topped by an octagon with clerestory windows. A library on the opposite side repeated the octagon at a smaller scale. The horizontal flow of the plan gave continuous, changing vistas through open passageways. Constructed around a large willow tree, the Studio became known as the house with the tree growing through it, adding to Wright's local reputation for eccentricity.

The ambience was pure then and future Wright — oak leaves and wild and dried flowers in handcrafted pottery and copper containers; tall, slatted wood benches and chairs, softened with cushions, before huge brick fireplaces; Japanese prints displayed on Wright-designed easels; and an eclectic range of statuary from reproductions of the Winged Victory of Samothrace and the Venus de Milo (both of which appeared and reappeared strategically in Wright interiors) to Beaux Arts nymphs.

The artful sentimentality and somber earth tones would seem old-fashioned to later eyes, but the open plan with its shifts in perception and the transforming simplicity of his style were radically new to late-nineteenth-century sensibilities accustomed to elaborate rooms smothered in portieres and picturesque clutter. Wright rejected the clutter, but his modernity, as bare as it seemed at the time, was still evocatively picturesque in the nineteenth-century tradition. His style was a balancing act between romantic naturalism and geometric abstraction. He never left the natural world out of the design equation, but decorative details derived from nature were increasingly rendered in simplified, geometric terms. He was not an admirer of the fin de siècle sinuousities of art nouveau. The straightedge, the triangle, and the compass were his tools; the intriguingly complex patterns of circles, squares, triangles, and hexagons that these tools produced made up his preferred design vocabulary. The passage of a century and the advent of minimalism and computer-aided geometry have dimmed the radical edge of Wright's work; seen in context, and by his contemporaries, it was shockingly unconventional.

What made the construction of the Studio possible was a contract with Luxfer Prism; in return for using and publicizing the special light-refracting qualities of a new kind of glass, Wright received a retainer that provided the necessary funds. The Studio not only added essential drafting space, it also acted as a more professional showcase for his taste and talents. He lost no time in following other approved routes for contacts and exposure, joining professional groups and civic committees, giving lectures, and participating in architectural exhibitions. He was one of the early members of the Chicago Arts and Crafts Society, which represented the leading edge of the arts in the 1890s. His work was featured in the annual exhibitions of the Chicago Architectural Club in 1894 and 1895, and was so prominently displayed in 1898, in rooms of his own design, that there were protests about what some considered an unseemly aggressiveness in taking over the show. His contribution in 1899 was considerably scaled back, but enemies had been made — a practice that he did not avoid and even seemed to encourage in later years. The passion that consumed him and occasionally supported him, his love and assiduous collecting of Japanese prints, was to lead to an exhibition of his finest at the Art Institute of Chicago in 1906 and, again, in 1908.

Jane Addams's Hull House, the center of Chicago's liberal culture, was the site of Wright's lecture on "The Art and Craft of the Machine" in 1901, a talk that broke ranks with the reformers of the arts and crafts movement who had rejected machine manufacture for a return to handcrafts. With the encouragement of magazines, books, and charismatic cultural gurus, an affluent America with time for higher things had produced a flood of art pottery, hand painting and weaving, block printing and handmade papers and books, and the infinite busywork of ladies' home arts. Although crafts were a considerable part of Wright's aesthetic arsenal, he maintained that technology was an essential partner for architecture. He called for the proper understanding and use of the new industrial materials, steel and reinforced concrete. Speaking on "The Architect" a year earlier, before a meeting of the Architectural League of America, he had called for a new architecture to suit the times. This remained his persistent theme. His own work had begun to be published in professional journals by admiring editors. None of this activity hurt his prestige. He was perceived not only as a rising young professional with interesting ideas, but also as a leader of the architectural culture of the day and a connoisseur and patron of the arts.

The decade from 1895 to 1905 saw the birth of three children to the growing family — sons David and Robert, born in 1895 and 1903, and a daughter, Frances, in 1898, joined Lloyd, John, and Catherine. He completed almost forty houses and two major commissions, Unity Temple in Oak Park and the Larkin Company Administration Building in Buffalo, New York.

The buildings of this period would stand as icons of American architecture even if Wright had never done anything else. What they all have in common is a strong original vision and a faultless eye for scale and detail. In addition, the Prairie house represented a domestic revolution. Wright laid out his concept in the *Autobiography* in terms anyone could understand, with a set of instructions that deconstructed the existing American home. Get rid of the attic, he commanded, and the dormer, and the cramped little rooms behind the dormers that housed the help. (That act, alone, which brought the servants out of the attic, was a social revolution.) Eliminate the basement. Replace multiple tall chimneys with one or two broad ones, and keep them low, on gently sloping or flat roofs. Start the house at ground level, with the cement or stone water table as a platform. Stop the walls at the second story for a continuous band of windows at bedroom height, sheltered by broad eaves. Make the hearth and fireplace the defining, unifying, center of the house.

Take a human being for scale, he insisted, bring down ceilings and doors to a human height. (They seem low now, but he was responding to the lack of domestic intimacy in high-ceilinged Victorian houses.) Wright took himself, at a slightly stretched 5 feet 8½ inches, as measure, which made problems for taller occupants.

He was unmoved by complaints. Treat the wall as a "screen," not as "the side of a box," freeing space, rather than confining it. Turn the living areas into a single open space where functions flow into one another with minimal demarcation. No more "boxes inside boxes called *rooms*." Allow the spaces to swing around the central hearth, or to project out into the landscape. Simplify, rather than elaborate. Make the plan and the setting come together as an organic, natural whole.

This was architecture as something distinctly new — as sociology, environment, and art. In the words of Grant Manson, author of an irreplaceable study of this early work, *Frank Lloyd Wright to 1910: The First Golden Age*, what Wright had achieved was the "electrifying reorientation of the American dwelling." The Prairie house could be "simple or complex"; it was suitable for "palace or cottage" and could be built of "durable stone or light frame, sided in stone, brick, stucco or brown shingles, set in forest or manicured lawn." With their interlocking volumes and intersecting spaces, their counterpoint of dynamism and serenity, the Prairie houses were as beautifully massed and proportioned as any classical villa. The critic and historian

Reyner Banham, writing in 1969, called Wright "America's greatest architect to date and the world's best domestic architect since Andrea Palladio."

The Prairie house type was established as early as 1900 in the B. Harley Bradley and Warren Hickox houses in Kankakee, Illinois, and the Ward Willits house of 1902–1903 in Highland Park. The William Winslow house of 1893–1894 that preceded them in River Forest had a long, low Roman brick base topped by a deep band of patterned tile below the shadowed overhang of a hipped roof. This was the last of Wright's houses to have double-hung windows. "No more holes punched in walls," he decreed. The symmetrical design and center entrance were also never to be repeated. The formal street façade is strikingly handsome; the less visible sides accommodate more specialized domestic functions.

But Wright's family-oriented hearth and home design would be brutally ruptured by changing twentieth-century social realities. And his combination of prescience and reaction was to lead to an anachronistic stance responsible for many of his later problems with European modernism. His Emersonian belief that all art was linked to nature and infused with spiritual and religious values was increasingly at odds with the pragmatism of the stripped-down functionalist aesthetic and industrial model of the International style. Some of the leading European practitioners visited him and his work; Mies van der Rohe was welcomed at Taliesin, but Le Corbusier and Walter Gropius were rejected when they made overtures. He would treat them publicly as the enemy, reinforcing his isolation from the mainstream.

Wright's fame and skill were growing rapidly, and whatever claims he made to a superior, maverick position, he was no longer an outsider. His Chicago and Oak Park connections had contributed to his acceptance by young, affluent, artistic, and intellectual clients. His own office was well established, and he was about to receive an extraordinary proposition. His work had come to the attention of Daniel Burnham, the distinguished Chicago architect who was the guiding spirit of the White City of the 1893 world's fair. They moved in intersecting circles of successful businessmen and patrons of the arts. The Wrights were invited to dinner at the home of a mutual acquaintance, Edward C. Waller, who apparently believed, with Burnham, that the young man was exceptionally talented, but that his talent was misdirected. As Wright recounted the story in the *Autobiography*, he was escorted into the host's library after dinner, where the door was locked and a rather startling private conversation took place over coffee and cigars. Burnham offered to send Wright to Paris for the three-year course at the Ecole des Beaux-Arts, since Wright had no formal architectural education, and then to the American Academy in Rome for another two years. He would pay all expenses, and take care of Wright's wife and children during that time. On Wright's return, Burnham promised him a partnership in his firm. It was an amazing offer, carrying a guarantee of a prestigious career.

Wright refused. If pure, personal ambition had been all that fueled him, he would never have turned the offer down. If success were all that mattered, Burnham's proposition would have been instantly accepted. If he was being arrogant, he never pretended to be anything else; he believed completely in himself, his work, and his ideals. If he was as opportunistic and unprincipled as some insist, his reaction is the telling incident of his character and career. Any other young architect would have jumped at the chance to study at the finest schools in Paris and Rome and become a partner in one of the country's best firms. Wright's integrity was a flexible thing, depending on opportunity and desire; he could rationalize almost anything if it suited his interests, but this put his innermost beliefs, everything he had constructed, to the test.

It is important to remember how impressive and influential Burnham was in the architectural and social worlds of the time. Wealthy and well-connected, his position and his credentials were impeccable. His Chicago office vied with Adler and Sullivan's in size, importance, and commissions, but his establishment firm outclassed the partnership of an Irishman and a German Jew. The offer was a solid gold sinecure, the certain route to the top and a world of privilege and prestige. There would be no creditors, no lack of all those necessary luxuries, no need to ever struggle again.

The reason he could not go, Wright explained, was that Sullivan had "spoiled" the Beaux Arts for him. He considered the classical tradition in which Burnham worked an impediment to creativity. Trying to express his thoughts to what must have been a silent and astonished group of important and confident men, he said he did not believe that this was the route to the best and most meaningful kind of building that this country could produce. "I saw myself influential, prosperous, safe," he later wrote, "with Daniel H. Burnham's power behind me. . . . I felt like an ingrate. Never was the ego within me more hateful than at that moment. But it stood straight up against the very roof of my mind. . . . This was success? . . . I'd rather be free and a failure. . . . I'm going on as I started. . . . I'm spoiled by birth, by training, and by conviction. . . . I can't go, because I could never care for myself after that."

He cherished his image as a creative outsider. He would not be himself, or the person he fancied himself to be; the persona, real or invented, would be lost, traded for a safe and comfortable career. His championship of a new architecture would be subsumed by the predictable products of a traditional practice. The proposition was a Faustian bargain that he could not accept. Not least, although he did not say it, he liked the drama of being the star of his own show, his heroic stance of "truth against the world." He noted that

131

he did not tell Catherine about the offer until "long afterward."

At about this time, Wright began to use skilled cabinetmakers, glassmakers, and sculptors to carry out his designs. The Dana house in Springfield, Illinois, built for Susan Lawrence Dana in 1902–1904, was an elaborate showplace commissioned by the first of a line of intelligent, sophisticated, wealthy women who were attracted to Wright's stimulating ideas and persuasive personality. They invariably had strong ideas and tastes of their own and, since he was notoriously troublesome himself, things seldom ran smoothly. But he usually had his way, exercising complete control. There are fascinating progress pictures that show the old Dana home — a high, square Italianate villa, originally meant to be incorporated into the new construction — being surrounded and swallowed up by Wright's walls and eventually demolished.

The Dana house had clear glass windows with colored and leaded accents executed by Orlando Giannini, a gifted glassmaker who would continue to produce windows in many intricate and beautiful patterns for other commissions. Wright's windows are so prized by collectors that his houses have been vandalized for them, and some owners have deliberately removed them for sale. Furnishings of this period attract stratospheric prices. The Dana house windows had designs of wild sumac, reduced to a stylized abstraction. Wright often used floral motifs; a stylized hollyhock would symbolize one of his most famous California houses, built for another of these wealthy, demanding women, Aline Barnsdall.

Painted friezes filled the lunettes of the Dana house's barrel-vaulted dining room, reminiscent of the Oak Park Playroom. The interior wood was oak; the colors, from brown to bronze, were warm but somber, with gold and copper accents. Pottery, tiles, furniture, carpets, and hangings were all custom-made to Wright's designs. Tables, chairs, lamps, and accessories were solid and straight-lined. Wright's unrelentingly upright, right-angled furniture was a perennial cause of client complaint; most learned to live with it. A statue of stylized romantic aspirations and dimly suggestive sexuality, *The Flower in the Crannied Wall* — the name taken from Tennyson's poem — was executed by one of Wright's favorite sculptors, Richard Bock. Moved later to a garden at Taliesin, it has been subjected by scholars to obscurely complex, symbolic analysis.

Given the resources, confidence, and liberty provided by moneyed clients, Wright was able to dictate every detail, inside and out, even designing clothes for the women to wear; an elegant tea gown seemed to be the preferred garment. Photographs show suitably attired clients, or clients' wives, in their Wright-designed and -furnished homes, posed next to masses of leaves and Japanese prints hung by, and probably bought from, Wright. Social position was still equated with elaborately furnished and gilded gloom; Wright's rooms, even with their dark wood and autumnal colors, swept it all away. And while they owed something to the domestic revolution in Britain in the houses of C. F. A. Voysey and Edwin Lutyens, they were quintessential Wright. A few have been rescued as owners and tastes changed; the living room of the later Francis Little house in Wayzata, Minnesota, was installed in the Metropolitan Museum in New York when the house was demolished, where it retains a timeless, disembodied, Wright-charged presence.

The Darwin D. Martin house in Buffalo, New York, was also built for a client willing and able to provide design freedom. The Martin brothers, Darwin and William, successful manufacturers of stove and shoe polish, became lifelong clients and friends who bore Wright's escapades and inconstancies with affection and forbearance and timely infusions of cash. Darwin Martin's house was connected to a conservatory by a 100-foot-long pergola, which provided a dramatic vista of plants and flowers from the entrance hall. A superb wisteria mosaic was a gleaming presence over the entry hall fireplace, and the leaded casement windows with accents of green, white, and gold, were, again, by Giannini. In 1937, two years after Darwin Martin died, his widow moved out and the empty house was systematically and ruthlessly gutted by his son, Darwin R. Martin, who cared nothing for it, or that "rascal," Wright, and undoubtedly resented his father's extended aesthetic and fiscal captivity. He stripped and cannibalized the house of its doors, windows, moldings, lighting fixtures, and wiring to reuse them in other investment properties he owned, after removing and disposing of all the furnishings. Left unlocked and vulnerable to random acts of thievery and violence for the next seventeen years, the house was vandalized continually, with the damage compounded by Buffalo's notorious winter weather.

The city of Buffalo acquired the house for back taxes in 1946, and a nominal caretaker was installed who simply presided over the continuing destruction. The derelict house was bought by an architect, Sebastian Tauriello, in 1954, who restored and furnished it in a 1950s fashion for his family and office. Tauriello loved the house but he was not a wealthy man; to make his purchase economically feasible, he created rental apartments in the twenty-room house and sold a piece of the property for an apartment building behind it, demolishing the badly deteriorated pergola and garage. It was not a historic restoration; this was a courageous, expeditious, and purely functional adaptation of a building in terminal decay. Tauriello literally saved the Martin house. After his death in 1965, his widow sold the house to the State University of New York at Buffalo, to be used as a residence for its president, Martin Meyerson, a Wright admirer, who undertook a partial restoration. Meyerson's successor moved out, and the house languished, with only emergency repairs. As structural studies and cost estimates proceeded doggedly through the 1990s, a serendipitous visit by Senator Daniel Patrick Moynihan, an ardent architecture buff, turned the tide. Shocked to find the building closed because of minor thefts and continuing deterioration, he obtained publicity and funding. The Darwin D. Martin house was finally secured after one of the longest-running dramatic cliffhangers in preservation history.

Two other buildings, the Larkin Administration Building of 1902–1906, also in Buffalo, and Unity Temple, built in Oak Park in 1905–1908, are among Wright's finest and most original works. The Larkin Building was designed for a mail-order soap company; like many of Wright's designs, which he always claimed he could just "shake out of his sleeve," it appears to have been almost instantly conceived in its main plan and features. It was Wright's custom to think through a design so thoroughly before putting it on paper that he could develop it with astonishing speed. The Larkin Building's massive brick structure bore little resemblance to comparable commercial construction. Glass entry doors led to an unexpected explosion of space and light within the solid brick walls; the surprising interior was a five-story court, a huge, open volume surrounded by balconies with a skylight above. To leave the space uninterrupted, the stairs were placed in corner towers joined to the main mass by slender glass light slots. The monolithic exterior was given scale and proportion by a pattern of vertical piers and suppressed horizontal floor slabs that expressed the balcony levels. An unornamented cornice and sculpture-topped piers emphasized the building's powerful geometry. The stripped, articulated volumes suggest the work of Josef Maria Olbrich and Otto Wagner in Austria, both of whom Wright admired and whose work he was familiar with through publications.

The Larkin Building's conceptual strength and creative confidence are still stunning. Wright stressed its many "modern" features — an early air-conditioning system, special lighting, metal files and office furniture of boldly original configuration. It was a spectacular concept, handsomely executed, an extraordinary structure for the offices of a mail-order company. One suspects that the vast, open space with its metal fittings was probably noisy. Still, filling mail orders may have been a reasonably quiet occupation; an organ played soft background music. The sound may have turned into a gentle murmur as it rose. In any event, these considerations wouldn't have bothered Wright. Photographs of the interiors taken at the time of completion show long-skirted women workers in pompadours and Gibson girl blouses. The building seems at once futuristic and old-fashioned, like something out of a retro *Star Wars*.

The Larkin Building received instant, international notice; it was generously published and written about in the contemporary architectural press. Admired and studied abroad, it was visited by C. R. Ashbee from Britain and Hendrik Berlage from the Netherlands as part of a growing overseas exchange among the practitioners of an evolving modernist style. The building was less well received at home. A leading architecture critic, Russell Sturgis, put off by its stark monumentality, called it ugly, and many agreed. After it outlived its usefulness, the structure stood empty for many years, and was finally torn down by the city of Buffalo in 1950, an act of destruction subsequently recognized as cultural vandalism.

Unity Temple suffered delays because of its unusual construction, something that has been true for unconventional or innovative architecture in almost any time or place. The budget did not allow for expensive masonry, and Wright decided to build the church, commissioned by Oak Park's Unitarian congregation, in cast reinforced concrete, a new and experimental material being pioneered for automobile plants in Detroit by the architect Albert Kahn, and for industrial construction in California by the engineer Ernest L. Ransome. Wright, as usual, was attracted to the newest developments; he was clearly intrigued by the possibilities of an unprecedented kind of monolithic construction, and its suitability for the geometric forms he favored. Conceived as quickly and totally as the Larkin Building, the church consisted of two sections, a cube containing the auditorium, its volume defined by exterior piers, and a connected, rectangular parish house, characterized as a "good time place" by Wright. Never given to understatement, his presentations were always long on lyrical descriptions and extravagant promises that masked his more serious intentions.

The apparent simplicity of the cube was deceptive — it was actually a Greek cross within a square, with seating and circulation on several levels. The square always had a symbolic, almost mystical significance for Wright. Like Froebel blocks put together, the heights of the cubed volumes varied, with the highest skylight directly above the central cross and auditorium. Other ceiling heights stepped down over the arms of the cross, where banks of windows fronted by the pilasters that topped the solid walls admitted light from the sides. The rough concrete walls, with the marks of the daily pours, have been softened over time by vines. But the interior is unchanged; its wood-banded walls and Wright-designed fittings and its subtly modular composition create a measured setting of serenity and repose. Wright has been accused of simply wanting to build this design, for any purpose he could justify. In a sense, that is true; all architects adapt their best ideas to the problem at hand; they all have favorite concepts that they explore, repeat, and revise. The open cube with its layered spatial richness is "a noble room for worship," as he intended. And it is something more — a humanistic concept that needs no conventional religious forms or symbolism to express the ideal the congregation requested — the unity of God and man.

The building that is considered by many to be Wright's Prairie house masterpiece, the Robie house, in Chicago's Hyde Park, was built in 1908–1910 for Frederick C. Robie, a bicycle manufacturer and auto parts supplier who was an early enthusiast of the automobile — an interest shared by Wright, who was already ordering fancy custom cars. Robie was only thirty in 1906, when he came with sketches and a vague idea of what he wanted; in an interview published fifty years later, he remembered that contractors and architects to whom he had spoken had all said, "I know what you want, one of those damn Wright houses!"

The design and construction of the house are described in evocative detail by architectural historian Joseph Connors. Built on a suburban corner lot among conventional nineteenth-century homes, the Robie house, he writes, "confounds expectations of what a house should look like. It has no street façade and no obvious door. There are hardly any solid walls. It seems to be a building assembled out of giant blocks, free-floating roofs, and endless ribbons of windows." What one sees is an "interwoven image" of "balconies and roofs that appear to have hurtled past each other in a near collision course."

The main mass of the three-story brick

and stone structure contains an enormous, continuous open area that serves as living room, dining room, and study; this "single room type," as Wright called it, is broken only by a connecting fireplace sunk low in the floor. The horizontality was further emphasized by the long front balcony, with waist-high windows and glass doors, and the cantilevered roofs above. The entrance, at ground level, is not on the street, but at the rear. This ground floor was devoted to a billiard room (Wright seemed to think everyone should have one) and a children's playroom, with stairs leading up to the living area above. Guest quarters, a kitchen, and servants' rooms were tucked into a wing behind the main volume. Bedrooms were on the third floor, under the roof's sweeping overhang.

Frederick Robie lived in the house only two years before his marriage and his business failed. The building has survived under the erratic stewardship of the University of Chicago, although its landmark status is assured. Wright scholar Neil Levine calls it "the most elaborate, extreme, and conclusive expression" of Wright's Prairie house — a distinction Thomas S. Hines believes should be shared with the Coonley house built in 1906–1909 in Riverside, Illinois. But it was the last that he built before he abandoned his Oak Park practice, turning the house's completion over to others, before embarking on the first scandalous chapter of his relentlessly scandalous life.

The collegial arrangement of marital and professional togetherness that he had conceived as a utopian way of life had become a pressure cooker of domestic and professional responsibilities. A staff had to be fed and paid. With strong wills and minds of their own, the children were constantly underfoot. Catherine started a kindergarten on Froebel's principles, adding more children to the chaos. Creditors came in person and by post. Patience and tempers wore thin, with frequent quarrels and a growing estrangement between husband and wife. The children — Lloyd, in particular — took their mother's side, much as the young Frank had done at the time of his parents' divorce. Wright became acutely aware of his lack of paternal instincts; he knew he was not a good family man. He never fancied himself in the role of father; he confessed in his memoirs that he hated the sound of "pa-pa." They were all so young, he said later; he felt as if they were children together. He was more like a

144

delightful and playful uncle, when he had the time. After extensive *mea culpas* of this sort, he managed to come out on top of his guilt or regret. Work was his life, his buildings were his children, he confessed in the *Autobiography*, although it was less confession than something he simply accepted as fact. "The architect absorbed the father," he concluded, which, in his mind, seemed justification enough.

When the stresses became unbearable, he could not work. He wrote to Darwin Martin that he had lost his accustomed energy and optimism and was unable to deliver plans he had promised. This went beyond his customary charming delinquency; he was deeply depressed. His life had always been in precarious balance, but now it was out of control. He had established himself as a successful architect with a substantial, suburban lifestyle among clients and friends who were the most progressive and prosperous members of the community. This would have been enough for any other man. But it was all coming apart for Wright; domestic and financial problems overwhelmed him, and the model of life and work that he had aspired to, and attained, was about to collapse. It was 1909, and by his own account, he was not quite forty, although he had actually passed that landmark two years earlier. He was having a midlife crisis of monumental proportions. Unable to resolve his multiple obligations, he was about to set a standard for spectacularly shocking behavior. "Because I did not know what I wanted," he wrote later in the *Autobiography*, "I wanted to go away."

He had actually known what he wanted for some time. He wanted to go abroad, to see at first hand the European work that he admired, to visit the countries and the cities where the exciting innovations were taking place. Above all, he wanted out of his life, to escape, to be somewhere else. In the fall of 1909, he left, abruptly cutting all ties. He abandoned a wife and six children and closed his practice, leaving debts and unfinished projects behind. Among the unpaid bills was the usual oversize one for groceries, for almost $900; this was something his son Lloyd never forgot, along with the shock of being suddenly designated by his mother as the head of the family.

After attempts to hand over his work to his Studio associates failed, Wright gave it to a near total stranger, a Chicago architect named Hermann von Holst, who had little interest in, or ability to carry out, Wright's kind of design. Some projects were rescued by Marion Mahony, one of the earliest women graduates in architecture at MIT and a valued Studio member, who executed the superb Japanese-style renderings of Wright's houses that suggested nothing but serenity and control where chaos must have reigned. In a frantic rush of secret last-minute activity, he sold Japanese prints, borrowed money, and took off for Europe, with the explanation that his presence was urgently needed in Berlin for a portfolio of his work in preparation by a German publisher, Ernst Wasmuth. It must have seemed a heaven-sent excuse. But he did not go alone. His companion was Mamah Borthwick Cheney, the wife of Edwin Cheney, a couple for whom Wright had built a house five years earlier; she left her husband and two children to accompany him.

Infidelity is classic midlife therapy, and Wright undoubtedly found solace and pleasure in the attention and affection of an attractive and cultivated woman. The affair had apparently started while he was working on the Cheney house, as his marriage was disintegrating. Mamah Cheney was a college graduate who had been a librarian before her marriage; she spoke French and German, and was an admirer of the Swedish feminist Ellen Key, whose books had circulated among the Chicago intelligentsia. Catherine had become totally immersed in her children and the difficulties of running that ambitious and impecunious establishment. The pretty girl Wright married just out of high school, who bore him so many children that the joke ran that he was unable to identify them when asked to do so quickly, had neither the time nor the desire to keep up with his rapidly broadening world. She had joined literary groups and social causes as part of their joint community role, but it seems that she did not share his interests at the same level of knowledge and intensity. In later years, she became a social worker; she never sought a profession in the arts. There were conflicts of priorities, and bitter disagreements. Inevitably, the two withdrew into their own hostile worlds. Wright and Mamah Cheney had done little to hide their affair. Both Catherine and Edwin Cheney knew, and it was common gossip even before their departure made it tabloid news.

The story is told that an enterprising reporter found a Frank Lloyd Wright and wife registered at the Hotel Adlon in Berlin; whether he was tipped off or simply curious, his discovery was on the front page of all the suburban and Chicago newspapers. Architects were good copy. When Stanford White was shot and killed by Harry K. Thaw over his mistress, Evelyn Nesbit, in 1906, it was a circulation-sustaining story. Wright's shocking behavior supplied columns of titillating, outraged, and lurid commentary. The manner of his departure and the desertion of his family inspired vitriolic moral tirades — he was condemned from the pulpits of churches and labeled a sinner and social outcast. He wore the mantle of shame lightly, and the course he followed in future years did nothing to reinstate him; it was a role he came to accept and eventually enjoy. His justification for his actions served to excuse the unrepentant pursuit of an unconventional life. As he explained often and untiringly, morality is in the mind of the beholder, and in his mind, morality had a higher meaning of his own definition. Faced with a choice between personal freedom and marital slavery, one must choose freedom, he said, quoting Ellen Key's statement that marriage "is not bondage"; to hide one's true feelings would be unworthy. Surely he was not at fault; the culprit was society's hypocritical attitudes. Or to put it another way: adultery as "truth against the world."

Historians and biographers have speculated ever since about the reasons behind Wright's departure. It seems clear enough in retrospect: a marriage gone bad, a houseful of disturbing and destructive children — he noted the endless interruptions and that things were always breaking — for whom his paternal feelings were limited, an overload of work in a smothering home-studio arrangement, ever deepening financial troubles, pressure and exhaustion that fed his inability to deal with escalating problems beyond his control. Underlying his personal unhappiness was something deeply, disturbingly important to him — the conviction that he had reached the end of the line, that he had done all he could with domestic architecture, that he needed to find a way to move on. This sense of an impending professional dead end overshadowed everything else; it was the final, overwhelming spur to action.

Among the distinguished visitors to the Studio was Kuno Francke, professor of the history of German culture at Harvard, who made it clear that Wright must visit Europe, and Germany in particular, to become part of the new international architecture. Wright, characteristically, claimed that Francke told him that Europe was ready for his contributions and America was not. The catalyst for his discontent, and the event that made flight possible, was the contract with Wasmuth — Wright knew the portfolio would be of great importance to his career. Artistic ego and ambition overrode any normal sense of obligation to family, staff, and clients. Dereliction of duty meant far less to him than his passionate and consuming need to renew his creative energies, to move to a new level of work and achievement.

The stress in the home and the Studio must have been tangible and demoralizing. An assistant remembered a visit from Henry Ford, brought by his son, Edsel, who knew Wright's reputation, to discuss the design of a suitable estate for the new millionaire, and Wright's dismal failure to project his usual convincing charm and enthusiasm. Although a house was designed by Wright's gifted associate, Marion Mahony, Ford never built it.

A final blow was the loss of an almost completed project for Harold F. McCormick, the Chicago agricultural-machinery heir, and his wife, Edith, the daughter of John D. Rockefeller. Wright was finishing the final landscape drawings when Edith McCormick rejected the plans. The McCormick project would have signaled Wright's personal and professional acceptance at the highest level of Chicago society, something he undoubtedly coveted. The loss of the commission must have been particularly galling because Edith McCormick went instead to Charles Platt, a New York architect who specialized in classical villas for the wealthy members of the Eastern establishment — a style and a clientele Wright professed to despise. Under different circumstances his disappointment would not have lasted; he would have gone on to other projects. Under these conditions, it was a crushing blow.

It is clear that Wright had reached a plateau, a dangerous and debilitating point in his life and career. The achievement of the Prairie houses was past, and the style was being widely copied by others; a successful Prairie school had grown up around him, but its younger members no longer acknowledged or wanted his leadership or example. He had made as many enemies as friends. For the artist, the focus on self, on personal development and artistic destiny, is a drive that excludes everything else. Normally endowed people living normal lives see it as inexcusable selfishness. Wright possessed more than the usual quota of talent and narcissism. He would have acted on his instincts and followed his own path, in any event, but his action was spurred by an insupportable situation. And he had fallen in love with another woman — a classic route to another life. He made a conscious decision in 1909 to leave it all, to abandon twenty years of work and marriage. This was the year, he later wrote in the *Autobiography*, that "The Road Closed."

6

It was not pure romantic passion, although he asked Catherine for a divorce and proclaimed his intent to marry Mamah when she was free (her husband quickly and quietly completed that legal step), or sinful lust, as the newspapers whipped up the story with prurient glee, or his unfailing instinct for drama, as some have speculated, that inspired Wright's exodus. It had as much to do with his priorities as artist and architect and the single-minded pursuit of his own potential, as with the crisis in his personal life.

Since no attempt had been made to hide the affair, it could have been no surprise when Mrs. Cheney went with him. He was a man who liked women and would always have one by his side. Driving married clients around in the flashy automobiles he favored was one of the many things he did of which his Oak Park neighbors disapproved. "He was a victim of women," a friend later wrote in a letter quoted by biographer Robert Twombly, "they took up more of his time than really was necessary." He was easily and, apparently, willingly manipulated by them; the women he chose, or who more often chose him, had minds and agendas of their own. He was content to let them take over and manage the parts of his life that he preferred to ignore. That they invaded other parts inevitably followed; the complex mess of loves and lives that the pair created when they left Oak Park was dubbed by a Chicago newspaper, with more delicacy than most, an "affinity tangle." Wright managed to create affinity tangles for the rest of his life.

Mamah — born Martha, but always called Mamah — has remained a shadowy figure in most Wright histories. Her published pictures are not flattering and bear little resemblance to one another, but Taylor Woolley, the draftsman who shared the villa in Italy where the work on the Wasmuth portfolio was done, remembered her as one of the loveliest women he had ever known. She was thirty when she married Edwin Cheney, a popular Chicago businessman, an age every woman of her generation, brainy or beautiful, approached with dread. She had accepted him on his third proposal, which does not suggest a match of passionate abandon.

Mamah's life did not revolve around her children as Catherine's did; she had other interests, and her attraction for Wright, overwhelmed and alienated by a child-centered household, was both physical and intellectual. She came with the kind of liberal ideas he admired; she believed, with Ellen Key, and as Wright would also proclaim, that one should pick one's partner "in harmony with one's own soul." Borrowing Key's language, undoubtedly supplied by Mamah, Wright announced that he and Mamah were "soul mates," that their "ideal love" transcended society's judgment. With his usual flexibility, Wright elevated infidelity to unassailable moral ground.

His women always came with intellectual and emotional baggage. One senses that he was more permissive than fanatical in the incorporation of their philosophies. His last wife, Olgivanna, with whom he shared the longest marriage and most enduring relationship, was a follower of Georgi Gurdjieff, whose philosophy and practices influenced the Taliesin Fellowship that Wright established in the 1930s, just as Key's beliefs colored his relationship with Mamah.

Mamah was a woman prepared to act on her ideals. She was determined enough, or infatuated enough, and certainly enterprising enough, to arrange a visit with her children to a friend in Colorado, and then to leave secretly for New York to meet Wright for the voyage, notifying her husband to collect the children in Colorado without revealing her plans. She was gone when he got there. She claimed later that if her sister had not agreed to come to Oak Park to care for the children, she would never have left them, although it is not clear whether that accommodation was arranged before or after her flight.

Much about Mamah has been revealed almost a century later in letters she wrote to Ellen Key during the European trip and after her return to America; they were found in the Royal Swedish Library by historian Alice T. Friedman, who published them in 2002. While she was with Wright, Mamah visited Key in Sweden, who treated her as an American "daughter." At that time, she made arrangements to become Key's official English-language translator, working first from German editions, and then learning Swedish to acquire exclusive publication rights for Key's treatise *Love and Ethics*. Mamah's emotional conflicts, her need for support and confirmation in seeking to live by Key's principles, were poured out in the letters to her mentor. In 1909, women's liberation was another half century away. The suffrage movement had so far succeeded in getting women the vote in only four states. Even the more daring women were just beginning to loosen their corsets and show their ankles, and hair would not be bobbed or skirts rise for another dozen years. Adultery was a serious moral offense, and a woman who abandoned her children was never readmitted to polite society. But Mamah's loyalty to Key never faltered; she blamed herself for doubts or emotional relapses. Later, there would be difficulties over numerous business and contractual problems, due to Key's suspicions about royalties as well as inconsistencies in her assignment of translation rights.

A good part of Mamah's time in Europe was spent away from Wright. After some weeks together in Berlin and Paris, they parted; because she was fluent in French and German, she took a job teaching languages to German students at Leipzig University, and Wright settled into rented quarters in Florence to work on the Wasmuth portfolio. He was joined by his oldest son, Lloyd, now nineteen, and already an excellent draftsman, and Taylor Woolley, a draftsman from the Studio. The two would assist him with redrawing the buildings to uniform scale. Wright had asked Lloyd, at the time of his departure, to leave the University of Wisconsin to help him, arguing that the European experience would be more valuable than a university degree.

The three men set up their drawing boards in the living room of the small Villa Fortuna, where Wright had obtained the ground floor, warming their hands over charcoal braziers as the winter progressed, painstakingly producing the careful ink renderings on thin sheets of tracing paper required for publication. Wright traveled occasionally to Germany to see his publisher in Berlin and visit Mamah at Leipzig. By the spring of 1910, with the work largely complete, Wright moved to Fiesole, and Lloyd and Taylor Woolley left to travel through Europe, their expenses paid by Wright with his diminishing funds. Mamah rejoined him, united in "love and rebellion," as he put it, in the Villino Belvedere in Fiesole, "a little cream-white villa on the Via Verde," where the lovers shared long walks through flower-strewn hills by day and listened to nightingales in the moonlit pine woods at night. They returned to their "sanctuary," where a wood fire would be burning, or a small table with a white cloth would be set for two in a walled garden hung with yellow roses. Oak Park, the deserted wife, and meals with six strident children must have seemed a universe away from this exquisite setting of romantic intimacy. They traveled, visiting museums, galleries, and churches, until they were "saturated" with the beauty of monuments, paintings, and sculpture. During the stay in Fiesole, Mamah worked on the English translations of Key's writings, and Wright assisted, or at least advised. The American publication of the authorized edition of *Love and Ethics* in 1912 bore both "soul mates" names — Mamah Bouton Borthwick (she resumed her maiden name after her divorce) and Frank Lloyd Wright.

Wright's *Autobiography* contains a poetic tribute to the remembered pleasures of that summer. But the trip was far from a shared romantic idyll; he suffered periods of intense loneliness and depression. He recounts how he sat alone in a café in Paris on a gray and rainy January day, listening to a musician play Simonetti's *Madrigal*, something Lloyd had played on his cello accompanied by his father on the piano, during the days of family musicales. "The familiar strains gave me one of those moments of interior anguish when I would have given all I had lived to begin reliving the old strains again," he recalled. "The remembered music drove me out of the café into the dim streets of Paris with such longing and sorrow as a man seldom knows. . . . I wandered about not knowing where I was going, or how long . . ." But "it was not repentance," he was quick to add. "It was despair that I could not achieve what I had undertaken as Ideal." Not regret, not guilt, not pain for himself or others; he had managed, as usual, to convince himself that his only fault was that he had aimed too high and fallen short of the mark.

Wright's version of events was meant less to disguise his own faults than to serve his single-minded pursuit of an artistic vision and the obsessive desire to build. Those who change the course of art use any means to convince the world that it needs something it neither anticipates nor understands and rarely wants. Artistic achievement is in large part a function of will; it is rarely a function of character.

Critics and writers intent on exposing and condemning lapses in behavior and judgment have turned themselves inside out trying to separate personal morality from the art produced. In the end, it is the art that endures.

Wright's defensive bravado in issuing bold statements in both his and Mamah's names (unlike his later lovers, she stayed discreetly in the background), proclaiming their dedication to personal and artistic freedom, succeeded only in outraging those they were meant to enlighten. Back in Oak Park, Catherine's statements were made with her minister at her side, as she avowed her enduring faith in her husband and her belief that he would return to his family. Pursued by an untiring and unrelentingly bottom-feeding press seeking new humiliations and sordid details, she radiated faith and optimism, declaring that her husband was battling demons within himself — struggling against the "vampire" with him; she knew he would win the fight. No, she insisted, there would be no divorce, or separation. He would do the right thing, and she and the children would be there for him when he came home. They would all be together again, as they were before. She was clearly determined to believe in her own version of events; it would be a dozen years before she released him and the divorce could finally take place.

For Wright the trip had a much larger purpose; he had business to attend to. There would be two publications: the large, two-folio *Ausgeführte Bauten und Entwürfe von Frank Lloyd Wright* and a smaller book of pictures and plans, with an introductory text by the English architect C. R. Ashbee, *Frank Lloyd Wright: Ausgeführte Bauten*, which he referred to as the *Sonderheft*, or special edition. He had decided to buy the books from Wasmuth, and part of the frantic predeparture fundraising had been devoted to finding a way to pay for them. As usual, a sympathetic client, Francis Little, stepped into the breach, providing a $10,000 loan with part of Wright's collection of Japanese prints as collateral. Wright finally sold the books himself, by mail.

But he was far less interested in profit than in positioning himself as the prophet and prime practitioner of a new American architecture. The publications were to make the case for "a pure art" that would be "the expressive vehicle of a pure society" — his buildings would be seen as a true representation of the progressive

163

American spirit. He was certain of his mission. He was, after all, part of a long line of preachers. His was the "cause conservative" — an architectural revolution based on the traditional values of family, hearth, and home. The fact that he had conspicuously violated these values in his personal life in no way invalidated the premise in his own mind, or the architecture that was its physical and spiritual vehicle. He had simply failed to live up to his own "Ideal."

The period of the European visit, from September 1909 to October 1910, and the time immediately following his return have been commonly referred to as "the lost years," a dark hole when little supposedly happened after the frenetic activity of the previous decades. The persistence of scholars has revealed that this time abroad was one of the most fruitful periods of Wright's life. He absorbed everything he saw — the cities and landscapes, the magnificent monuments and the modest vernacular, the great art of the past and the exciting innovations of a developing modernism pointing to the future. He later used it all, as he embarked on a new period of exploration and invention. The sense of sterility and fatigue were gone.

The recovery of that time, and an understanding of its significance, have been brilliantly reconstructed in Anthony Alofsin's *Frank Lloyd Wright — The Lost Years, 1910–1922*, a painstaking documentation and analysis of Wright's previously unrecorded activities. Subtitled *A Study of Influence*, the book describes the two-way cultural currents flowing across the Atlantic, and Wright's active participation in that vital exchange of ideas. Alofsin explodes Wright's carefully nurtured scenario of isolation and self-invention.

Like every architect who has ever visited Europe, Wright was an avid consumer of its treasures. He went to Berlin, Vienna, London, and to Paris twice. He took trips to the countryside and to small towns. He made pilgrimages to the new buildings he had seen only in publications or, in the case of Olbrich, sampled and studied with interest a few years earlier at the 1904 St. Louis World's Fair. He spent time in Olbrich's Secession Building in Vienna and made a special trip to Darmstadt to experience more of the architect's sensuous style. He admired Otto Wagner's Postal Savings Bank in Vienna, a brilliant reconfiguration of the classical tradition, completed a few years earlier. He studied Hendrik Berlage's striking 1890s Stock Exchange in Amsterdam and very likely knew about Berlage's recondite geometric theories of design.

He undoubtedly went to the exhibition rooms of the Deutsche Werkbund, which had opened in Berlin just two years before, in 1907, and visited the Wiener Werkstätte, in Vienna, where the latest designs for furniture and crafts were on view; he met the Werkstätte's founder, Josef Hoffmann. As early as 1900, the Secession exhibitions had included the latest German and Austrian products, and work from Scotland by Charles Rennie Mackintosh, as well as views of the rooms of the Maison Moderne in Paris by the Belgian architect Henri Van de Velde. The Academy was under attack and revolt and regeneration were in the air. After art nouveau, a more abstract and geometric style was appearing. Wright also discovered the ancient and indigenous cultures that the new art had embraced for their "unspoiled vision" as an antidote to the conventions of the Western tradition.

He acquired a painting and woodblock prints by Gustav Klimt, whose colorful, jeweled patterns must have appealed to him strongly, and discovered the sculpture of Franz Metzner, a proponent of "conventionalization," in which the human body was defined as a system of "conventions," or simplified, abstract forms. Wright later appropriated the theory for his own stylized treatment of figures and natural forms. One of the few design books he ever spoke of openly was Owen Jones's *Grammar of Ornament*, a history of decoration that emphasized the underlying geometry uniting all styles. Everything new propelled him from naturalism to abstraction, a dichotomy he would resolve in his own way. One of the myths promoted by Wright was that he was so well known abroad that the leaders of the new German modernism, Peter Behrens and Walter Gropius, were deeply influenced by his work. But it wasn't until the publication of the portfolio and monograph in 1911 that the details of Wright's buildings became widely available to those who had not made the trip to Chicago to see them.

In truth, the learning experience was largely his. And while it is generally known that a writer transforms experience into art, it is less well understood that an architect processes images in much the same way. Instead of reinventing the fabric of life as narrative, like the novelist, the architect is preoccupied with the look and nature of things in the physical world and how they translate into built form. All that Wright learned would be incorporated into the creative process, moving the art of building forward, advancing and changing the way architecture is experienced as a defining factor of life and place. This transformation is the indisputable basis of his genius, a word he never hesitated to apply to himself, usually preceded by the word "misunderstood."

He called the trip a "spiritual hegira" and "voluntary exile." But while escape and renewal were uppermost in his mind, he had also produced a definitive publication of his work and of the period, at a moment when its impact was particularly important for his career and the course of an evolving modern architecture. He had kept in touch with the jobs that interested him, sending sketches back to those conscripted to carry them out. In the back of his mind, he had no doubt that he would be able to return to a profitable practice, that he would, in his own words, "square my life with myself," finding exoneration on a personal and professional level. This would require all the guile and determination of which he was capable. Fortunately, he was well endowed with both.

By late summer of 1910, he had completed the work he came to do, and the money was running out. He was ready to return. He began to send out feelers and make plans. He had no intention of giving Mamah up, but he also understood that he must go back to Catherine, temporarily, at least; his personal situation had to be resolved. Whether he proceeded with a crafty and duplicitous plan, as some have suggested, or in his fashion, simply took it one step at a time, employing whatever mollifying or manipulative devices were necessary, his objective was always clear in his mind. He would return to the family for a while, resume his practice, and find a way to bring Mamah into his life.

He wrote to a friend and client, the Reverend William Norman Guthrie, for advice, adopting the role of rueful, repentant sinner, which he understood to be a prerequisite for his acceptance at home. Reentry, he knew, would not be easy in light of his transgressions. Guthrie's reply, preserved in the Frank Lloyd Wright Archives, delivered a laundry list of Wright's sins, which included abandoning his family, setting himself against the conventions of society by his adulterous behavior, and making matters worse by claiming a freedom from the "established order" and promoting unacceptable principles of love and marriage. Suggestions followed, most of which Wright ignored. He must return to his wife and children, declaring the affair at an end. He must renounce his endorsement of love without marriage. "There will never be a social order, I trust, in which cohabitation of any sort, physical or spiritual, will be prized over the discharge of parental duties," Guthrie wrote, reminding him of the social contract — we are not free, we have obligations to discharge, even at the cost of great personal sacrifice, and he was sure that Wright was capable of that sacrifice. He must conform to society's norms, not just for social acceptance, but because he would never be able to realize his full artistic potential by setting himself against them. Above all, he should not mention the writings of Ellen Key.

Having repented by correspondence, Wright sailed for home in October 1910, after a brief visit to his friend Charles Ashbee in England. Mamah did not go back until the following summer, when her divorce, obtained by her husband on grounds of desertion, became final; the wisest course seemed to be to keep her at some distance for a while, or at least to make her as inconspicuous as possible while he tried out the waters of Oak Park. The letter to Reverend Guthrie had done its work; received as an act of contrition, it prepared the way for his reappearance. Two days after landing in New York, he arrived in Oak Park; he had already contacted the ever-faithful brothers, Darwin and William Martin. William Martin was commanded to take Wright to the station for his luggage, which had been delayed, and when his wife refused to accompany him on the errand or to be seen in the company of the sinner, the somewhat chastened Martin took a route through back streets hoping no one would recognize them. Yes, Wright was really back, he reported in a letter to Darwin; he was his usual charming, confident self, dressed in tan sportsman's tweeds like "the fellow on the Quaker Oats package." He appeared to be neither conscience-stricken nor apologetic, and was apparently prepared to resume his life as before.

Wright knew, of course, that it would not be simple; there was the problem of his debts and the troubles at home and his future to be dealt with. He moved back in with Catherine, but he soon informed her that the marriage was over; he would have to make plans for the family's support and find another place to live. The Chicago and local papers, deprived of scandal except by repetition of the earlier events, stressed reports of the children's joy at having their father back.

The fall and winter of 1910 were spent trying to reestablish his practice and untangle his marital and financial affairs. There were design problems with the *Sonderheft* that he felt required his presence in Berlin, and in January 1911 he sailed for Europe again, returning a month later, after renegotiating his contracts with Wasmuth. Two interesting developments occurred that spring, timed so opportunely that there have been varying interpretations as to whether they were spontaneous or planned. One was his mother's purchase of land in Wisconsin's Helena Valley, and the other concerns Wright's intentions when she gave him the land and he developed plans for a house to be built there. As it turned out, the house was Taliesin, his great, emblematic, surpassingly beautiful home and studio. It was a home ever changing and evolving, the place closest to his roots, with the deepest meaning for his life and art.

Building Taliesin was probably his intention, and possibly his mother's, also; her continued presence in his life was a small price for the gift of the land. As determinedly possessive as ever, she would even condone his scandalous behavior and leave her own house near Catherine and the children in order to be with him. But the story Wright told was that Anna had bought some farmland "up country" for her return to Wisconsin to be near the family, and that he was about to build a "small house" for her. What makes the story suspect is that the extravagantly sentimental and expensive gesture of buying land at that moment was wholly out of character for this penurious and careful woman. Add to that the fact that the land she purchased happened to be Wright's favorite hill in the familiar valley, known and loved since his childhood summers working on Uncle James's farm. In addition, the early, more modest plans, begun six months after his return to the unhappy household in Oak Park, when he knew he must leave, contained a work area of considerable size and little apparent use to Anna; it seemed clearly destined for a studio.

He had to be thinking about where he would live and work. He was concerned about a place secluded enough to bring Mamah, where they could be together without constant curiosity and media surveillance. He also had to find a way to provide support for the family when he left. The solution must have been in his mind at the same time; he would remodel the Oak Park Studio for Catherine and the children as their home, leaving the house free for rental income to support them.

The "Anna" stratagem, however, worked perfectly for his purpose. He needed to borrow the money to carry out his plans, and a house for himself and Mamah would have been considered an offense against family and society. He was busy maintaining the fiction of the returned and repentant spouse who had given up the other woman. It was the ever indulgent Darwin Martin who was approached, and who ultimately succumbed to providing a construction loan, even agreeing to Wright's outrageous suggestion that he take on Anna's mortgage until her present house was sold.

Thanked, as usual, with enchanting effusions from the self-described unworthy but grateful recipient of this act of generous friendship that always followed such negotiations, Martin cheerfully termed himself not friend, but "sucker"; he would continue to accede to Wright's shameless financial requests for a loyal lifetime. And there would be a lifetime of such dodgy arrangements, since Wright's affairs were always in a hopeless snarl of indebtedness and overextension. Biographer Brendan Gill has called him, not without admiration, a consummate con man; one can only marvel at the panache and insouciance of his leveraged lifestyle. He operated with the stunning bravado of the man in the classic tale who is being sentenced for killing his parents and pleads for mercy from the court because he is an orphan. Still deeply in debt and with an uncertain future, Wright was about to build, not a small house, but a gentleman's country estate.

He is never more delightfully articulate than in the letters asking for advance payment from clients, or soliciting the loans that were often secured by the Japanese print collection. Later, during a particularly troubled period, the collection had to be sold at auction at a sacrifice price to satisfy the bank holding the Taliesin mortgage. But he always replenished it, keeping the prints in a stone vault in his studio, using them as a kind of cash reserve, selling them when he needed immediate funds. His activity as dealer and connoisseur of the art that both inspired and supported him is told fully by Julia Meech in her book *Frank Lloyd Wright and the Art of Japan: The Architect's Other Passion.*

As the plans progressed, the studio space became a drafting room, and the house grew until it enclosed three sides of the hill, surrounded by gardens, fountains, ponds, and a working farm. Located in Hillside, just across the Wisconsin River from Spring Green, Wright's home provided its own utilities and food supply, on 200 acres of rolling land. The way he conceived the house tells us more about his architecture than the most learned dissertations, of which there have been many. He describes it in the *Autobiography* not as a building but as a place in which nature frames and defines the dwelling, where the land and the views, the light and the seasons, the scents and colors, the plantings and the man-made insertion of native quarried stone and sand-toned walls are all part of a total, immensely sensuous and appealing design. His words are as eloquent and evocative as when he wrote them in the 1930s, recalling his vision of 1911. The house was, in fact, built for

Mamah, as well as for himself. He makes it clear that the dream included her at its center.

He visualized everything completely, beginning with the land, and all that he had learned of its beauties and bounties during those hard, hot summers on Uncle James's farm. "I saw the hill-crown back of the house as one mass of apple trees in bloom, perfume drifting down the Valley, later the boughs bending to the ground with red and white and yellow spheres. . . . I saw plum trees, fragrant drifts of snow-white in the spring, loaded in August with blue and red and yellow plums. . . . I saw the rows on rows of berry bushes, necklaces of pink and green gooseberries hanging to the underside of the green branches: saw thickly pendent clusters of rubies like tassels in the dark leaves of the currant bushes. . . . There were to be strawberry beds, white, scarlet and green. . . . I saw the vineyard on the south slope of the hill, opulent vines loaded with purple, green and yellow grapes . . . baskets filled to overflowing, to be set around the rooms like flowers. Melons lying thick in the trailing green on the hill slope. Bees humming over all, storing up honey in the white row of hives. . . . Sheep grazing on the upland slopes and hills. . . . Swans floating upon the water in the shadow of the trees. I looked forward to peacocks Javanese and white on the low roofs of the buildings or calling from the walls of the courts."

He would replicate the root cellar of his grandfather, in a modern version, "its wide sand floor piled high with squash and turnips, potatoes, carrots, onions, parsnips . . . apples, pears and grapes stored in wooden crates . . . all the cream the boy had been denied . . . it would float like an egg on the fragrant morning cup of coffee or ride on the scarlet strawberries. . . . Yes, Taliesin should be a garden and a farm behind a real workshop and a good home. I saw it all: planted it all: laid the foundation of the herd, flocks, stable and fowl as I laid the foundation of the house."

The vision soon mixes with an account of the details of the actual construction. Stone from a local quarry "went down for pavements of terraces and courts. Stone was sent along the slopes into great walls . . . stepped up like ledges on the hill . . . the hill-crown became a low-walled garden above the surrounding courts, reached by stone steps walled into the approach. A clump of fine oaks that grew on the hilltop stood untouched on one side

178

above the court. A great curved stone-walled seat enclosed the space just beneath them, and stone pavement stepped down to a spring or fountain that welled up into a pool at the center of the circle . . . the courts forming a sort of drive along the hillside flanked by low buildings on one side and by flower gardens against the stone walls that retained the hill-crown on the other." He devised a gravity-fed irrigation system that fell from a dammed stream to pools and fountains and watered the produce on the slopes.

He must have remembered the villas and farmhouses built into the Florentine hills. His perceptions of nature and building had been visibly enriched by his immersion in an older, European landscape and culture. The relationship of building to land is spelled out, its architecture defined. "Taliesin was to be an abstract combination of stone and wood as they naturally met in the aspect of the hills. . . . The lines of the hills were the lines of the roofs, the slopes of the hills their slopes, the plastered surfaces of the light wood-walls, set back into shade beneath broad eaves, were like the flat stretches of sand in the river below and the same in color. . . . Finished wood outside was the color of gray tree-trunks in violet light. Shingles of the roof surfaces were left to weather silver-gray like the tree branches spreading below them.

"Inside floors, like the outside floors, were stone-paved, or laid with wide, dark-streaked cypress boards. The plaster in the walls was mixed with raw sienna in the box, went onto the walls natural, drying out a tawny gold. . . . The rooms went up into the roof, tent-like, and were ribanded overhead with marking strips of waxed, soft wood. . . . Walls opened everywhere to views as the windows swung out above the treetops. . . . I wanted a house where icicles by invitation might beautify the eaves," he wrote. So there were no gutters. "Taliesin in winter was a frosted palace roofed and walled with snow, hung with iridescent fringes. . . . The whole low, wide and snug, broad shelter seeking fellowship with surroundings."

Construction proceeded rapidly in the summer of 1911, and by August the house was well enough along for Mamah to rejoin him on her return from Europe. It was not possible to keep her presence a secret for long, and soon wild press stories appeared about the sinful ménage; it was reported that Wright had been seen fording a stream carrying a woman in scanty European lingerie on his shoulders. The lovers were doing nothing more shocking than translating Key and Goethe. Mamah's children visited during the summer and school vacations. Her good manners and quiet charm were winning over local critics as she pursued normal activities and participated in community life.

Wright's work was also returning. The jobs given to Hermann von Holst on his departure for Europe were covered by a hastily executed contract that Wright now questioned. He became convinced that von Holst, and his own former associates, Marion Mahony and Walter Burley Griffin, who had completed the commissions, had stolen his clients, and he tried to reclaim the work still under way and collect fees that he felt were owed him. The matter had to be turned over to a lawyer, and after many months a settlement was negotiated in which Wright received the grand sum of $108.29. He had become embittered by what he saw as disloyalty and betrayal by former associates and friends, and was deeply resentful of a failure to credit him with the style that was now pervasive in the Middle West. With the exception of Taylor Woolley, he refused to rehire those who had worked with him before his departure.

The converted came willingly to Taliesin, although he was less accessible there than he had been in Oak Park or Chicago. By the spring of 1912, a half-dozen houses and a hotel were on the boards. He acquired an office in Chicago and a staff at Taliesin that included his son John and Woolley; a full schedule of jobs and exhibitions was under way. By early 1913, both Wasmuth publications were being distributed in America and quickly found their way into the libraries of Le Corbusier and other European modernists. He was receiving commissions for more complex buildings, far beyond his earlier domestic scale.

One of these larger undertakings was an entertainment complex in Chicago, Midway Gardens, modeled after German beer gardens. Meant to appeal to the city's large German community, it was to have both a winter garden and a summer garden, with restaurants and dance floors, and a concert shell, bandstand, and performance stage for traditional and popular entertainment. Wright created an enchanted fairyland with elaborate embellishment. The rich ornamentation included figures by the sculptor Richard Bock and his own designs for conventionalized "sprites" and stylized "muses in the manner of Metzner," interpreted and executed by another favorite collaborator, Alfonso Giannelli.

Inadequately financed from the start, Midway Gardens had a short, unenchanted life. It proved expensive to maintain and run, and was brought to an early end by Prohibition. After suffering many indignities by a series of owners trying to adapt it to other uses, it was demolished in 1929. Wright took a perverse pleasure, as he did later with the Larkin Building, in the fact that he had built it so well that it was extremely hard to tear down.

Wright's "spiritual hegira" and "voluntary exile" had turned the outsider into a social outcast. He had carried the independent, nonconforming tradition of the Lloyd Joneses past the point of no return by his rejection of the moral principles that were at its core. With his reentry into professional life, it now became necessary to create a self-justifying persona above censure. Not surprisingly, he had no trouble squaring his actions with divine truth as opposed to human hypocrisy. God had to be on his side. Wright remained a religious man, but that did not make him a charitable one. His growing belief that he had been bypassed, and even cheated, by those he had trusted, combined with his feelings of homage due but not delivered, fed resentments that were to reach near paranoid proportions. How much of this was truly felt, and how much was an effective act, is unclear. There was always a sense of amused self-knowledge behind the belligerent stance. One famous story tells of Wright being called to testify in a court case. Asked to identify himself, he announced that he was the world's greatest architect. When asked how he could make such a statement, he replied, with visible enjoyment and a gleam in his eye, that he had no choice, he was under oath.

By the spring of 1914, the design of Midway Gardens was complete, and after a frantic, four-month construction schedule, it opened to the public in June. Because it was still unfinished, Wright was spending much of his time on site with his son John; there were nights when he slept over — he said that his bed was a pile of wood shavings.

He was there, on August 15, 1914, when he received the traumatic news that tore his life apart. The press, always alert for disgrace or disaster, could not have invented a more tragic and terrible event. Everyone who was at Taliesin that day — Mamah, with her son, John, and daughter, Martha, who were visiting for the summer, two draftsmen from the studio, the Taliesin foreman and three workmen (a gardener, a carpenter, and the latter's son) — had been attacked with an axe by a deranged servant; seven had been hacked to death and the living quarters of Taliesin had been burned to the ground. Mamah's skull had been split with a single blow and the children killed next; her barely recognizable burned body was found where she died a few hours later. Three of the victims survived — one of the draftsmen, Herbert Fritz; the carpenter, William Weston; and the gardener, David Lindblom. Fritz had jumped through a window and broken his arm, but he was able to roll down the hill to smother his flaming clothes. Weston had been struck with the blunt end of the hatchet; somehow he and Lindblom, both bleeding and burned, ran a mile to the next house to call for help. Weston returned to find a hose in the garden wall, which he held on the fire until he was found and carried away. Some of the mortally wounded died almost instantly; others suffered for hours. The information that reached Wright in Chicago was only about the fire. He learned about the murders from journalists riding the same train back to Wisconsin, in hot pursuit of the story, probably already composing their leads about the bloody massacre in the "love cottage" Wright had built for his paramour. There would be descriptions, both grisly and mawkish, of the crime scene, and sermons on righteous retribution for sin. An ashen Wright had to be supported by his son John, who returned with him. Also on the train was Edwin Cheney, stunned by the deaths of his ex-wife and children. Husband and lover traveled together, united in shock and grief.

Wright had recently hired a couple from Barbados, Gertrude and Julian Carleton, as cook and houseman, on the recommendation of John Vogelsang, the owner of Midway Gardens. There are various explanations for what happened, none confirmed. Julian Carleton may have had a disagreement with a member of Wright's staff and been rebuked, and there was a rumor that Mamah, troubled by some display of temperament or insubordination, had planned to let the couple go. Whatever actually occurred, Carleton's violent response was psychotic; the man was clearly

186

insane. He had just served lunch, scrupulously correct in his white jacket, to Mamah and the children on a screened patio, and to the men in their dining room in another part of the house, when they smelled gasoline and saw a liquid pouring under the doors, which immediately burst into flames.

Most of the windows and doors of the dining room had been locked and, as the men tried to escape, their clothes and bodies ablaze, each was brutally bludgeoned by Carleton, standing behind the door. The scene found by the returning men was bloody carnage. The main part of Taliesin was a smoking ruin. A makeshift morgue was set up in a house nearby that Wright had built for his sister Jane and her husband, Andrew Porter, where the wounded were also carried. The moans of those who had not died instantly could be heard throughout the night. Wright also remembered hearing a whip-poor-will, a sound that would always evoke a terrible sadness. The search for Carleton, begun immediately, yielded nothing; he was found the next day hiding in the fire pit of the cold furnace. He had drunk acid, which had not killed him; taken to jail, unable to eat or speak, he died a month later.

In the morning, Wright's workmen made plain wooden boxes for the dead, and Edwin Cheney loaded one small box with the remains of his two children into a car for the return trip to Chicago. Mamah's body remained with Wright. The rest is best told in his own words, as he recorded the events in the *Autobiography*. "Black despair preceded a primitive burial in the ground of the family chapel. Men from Taliesin dug the grave deep. . . . I cut her garden down and with the flowers filled the strong plain box of fresh white pine to overflowing. My boy John, coming to my side now, helped lift the body and we let it down to rest among the flowers that had grown and bloomed for her. The plain box lid was pressed down and fastened home. Then the plain, strong box was lifted on the shoulders of my workmen as they placed it on our little spring-wagon, filled, too with flowers . . . we made the whole a mass of flowers. It helped a little."

Wright walked alongside the wagon to the chapel "where no bell tolled. No people were waiting." With the help of John and two young cousins, he "lowered the flower-filled and flower-covered pine box to the bottom of the new made grave. Then I asked them to leave me there alone.

I wanted to fill the grave myself. I remember the August sun was setting on the long familiar range of hills . . . then slowly, darkness. . . . I filled the grave, staying there in the dark.

"I saw the black hole in the hillside, the black night over all. . . . Days strangely without light would follow black nights. Totally — she was gone."

7

He put no headstone on the grave. Why mark the spot "where desolation ended and began?" he wrote in the *Autobiography*. "After the first terrible anguish," he could no longer imagine her presence, or feel her spirit. The horror of the event had numbed his senses — "the blow was too severe." He refused to let his mother come and sent his son away.

He slept in a small room behind the studio, the nights "filled with strange, unreasoning terrors. . . . The gaping black hole left by the fire in the beautiful hillside seemed a charred and ugly scar upon my own life — on all life." There are traumas too deep to deal with, guilt, real or imagined, too hard to face, losses too great to mourn. He suffered from boils on his back and neck. He thought he was going blind. After a while, he returned to the house he kept in Chicago and lived alone, with a housekeeper.

He vowed to rebuild Taliesin, and it was

the rebuilding that saved him. "In action there is release from anguish," he wrote. "Work only was bearable." He redesigned the places where the murders had taken place to exorcise memory. A new wing was built, with another great fireplace, and an outdoor stone loggia added that looked out to the Helena Valley. "Steadily, stone by stone, board by board, Taliesin II began to rise from the ashes of Taliesin I."

Every aspect of the tragedy had been exploited by the newspapers; those who knew nothing of his architecture knew everything about the scandals and sorrows of his personal life. Mail came from all over, much of it sympathetic. He said he tied the letters in a bundle, unread, and burned them; it is more likely that they were screened first by his staff. But there was one letter that he read and responded to, written in a tone of such sensitive understanding that he became curious about the sender. The writer was a wealthy divorcée, Maud Miriam Noel, who had been living in Paris as an expatriate and sculptor until the start of the First World War had forced her return. Miriam Noel, as she preferred to be known — she had dropped the old-fashioned Maud — was exactly the kind of cosmopolitan and "liberated" woman

Wright would find interesting and consoling, and he arranged to meet her at his Chicago office.

He was immediately intrigued. She was a worldly woman of forty-five, two years younger than he was, and far more attractive than he had expected. Like Wright, she was a master of self-image. Her dress was "artistic" in the current mode; she favored turbans, scarves, ropes of beads and furs adorning long gowns and wraps. She wore and played with a monocle as they spoke, smoked cigarettes, which he helped her light, and exuded an air of sophistication and mystery that was only heightened when she spoke of a "luckless" love affair, which immediately struck a symbiotic note with his own unhappiness.

Miriam Noel has been described as pretty, with an expressive face and large eyes. In photographs she is of average, rather than striking, appearance, round-faced, with eyes too close together for beauty; the softness of expression in early likenesses becomes grim and humorless in later pictures. She clearly cultivated personal drama. What Wright saw in her was a lively intelligence, a shared interest in literature and art, and a conviction, matching his, that they were above the crowd in their

aesthetic sensibilities. There were also inti-
mations of passion and the allure of the
eternal feminine mystique. She professed
to see in him genius, feeling, and taste.
What he did not see was that she took
drugs, was emotionally unstable and given
to wild mood swings, subject to unreasoning anger and irrational acts of vengeance. Only later did Wright perceive her
psychotic personality. Today she would be
considered schizophrenic. Her eccentricity
would escalate to the point where her behavior became so destructive and demoralizing that his life "seemed paralyzed by
subtle poison," he would write in the *Autobiography*. Most of all, as Neil Levine has
surmised so perceptively of this meeting,
"they saw in each other a companion in
misery."

They were, in fact, to make each other
miserable for the next seven or eight
years — the tie that bound them was a mu-
tually desperate need for love. Wright's
usual vulnerability to women was increased by what he himself called "a hor-
rible loneliness." When Catherine finally
agreed to a divorce, in 1922, Miriam Noel
became his second wife.

The affair began almost immediately.
Following an apparent night of ecstasy in

the Chicago house, Miriam wrote him a letter of postcoital ardor elevated to dramatic classical and literary heights, in which she addressed him as "Lord of my Waking Dreams." Citing Alcibiades and Agathon, she offered to crown him with violets and bind his hair with fillets of gold. She declared herself enslaved. "I kiss your feet," she wrote. "I am your prisoner." She would make his life a living hell.

Within the year, in the spring of 1915, Miriam moved to Taliesin. The relationship was stormy and troubled from the start. Shortly after the tragic events of 1914, Wright had written a grief-stricken piece in the local newspaper apologizing to his neighbors for the shock and horror they had been subjected to; after the usual defense of his personal morality, he expressed gratitude for their kindnesses to Mamah, and his hope for a life of tranquillity. The peace he hoped for never materialized. The press had a new scandal to savor.

Miriam was conspicuously present; unlike Mamah, who was silent while Wright sent forth pious statements about their unusual living arrangements, she joined him in proclaiming the singularity of their liaison. For those endowed with superior sensibilities, she announced publicly, the world must recognize a special status; they must be allowed to make and live by their own rules. Visitors to Taliesin were dazzled by her costume changes — she would appear in clinging white satin gowns or skimpy homespun robes, with headdresses to match; some were disturbed by her manipulative and controlling way of dealing with her lover. Wright seemed to be the one enslaved.

Their violent quarrels would ricochet from Wisconsin (an unlikely venue for Miriam, who was no Marie Antoinette playing at the bucolic life) to Japan and California; she went with him wherever he worked. Insanely jealous, she accused him of egotism, selfishness, and infidelity. He was incapable of loving anyone, she told him repeatedly, not the departed Mamah, nor the long-suffering Miriam; he loved only himself. She would bear his inhumanity and her own great love into the desert, alone.

When she would leave him after a particularly bitter fight, her tirades were delivered in long letters of devastating cruelty. He would abase himself in letters of equal hyperbole begging her to come back. Some of the letters, in which Miriam characterized his monstrousness in detail, were sent from her temporary refuge in the Chicago house, where they were intercepted by Wright's former housekeeper, Nellie Breen, whom he had apparently discharged. With a vengeance equal to Miriam's, she gave the letters to the newspapers, which had a field day with erotic character assassination. She then pointed out to interested officials that Wright had violated the Mann Act, which made it a crime to take females across state lines for immoral purposes. This curious legislation had been passed by Congress in 1910 in response to agitation about the "white slave" trade, in which prostitutes were forcibly taken from one state to another. Wright was charged, undoubtedly to the continuing delight of journalists who were making a career of his indiscretions, with the sinful and illegal act of taking Miriam from Illinois to Wisconsin. The law, used mostly for harassment, is still on the books, although it has been radically altered in its language to include both sexes and children, and to specify that the interstate traffic must be for criminal activity. Wright was the "luckless" one in this affair. He hired Clarence Darrow, the lawyer of the later Scopes "monkey trial," who had the charges dismissed.

Life with Miriam was no recipe for recovery from the events of 1914. The one thing that she perceived correctly was that his devotion to Mamah had not died with her; she saw Mamah, still, as a formidable competitor for his loyalty and love. What rescued him from the trauma of Taliesin — if not from the ordeal of Miriam, whose persecution of the lord of her waking dreams continued for years after the relationship ended — was the commission for the Imperial Hotel in Tokyo, which took him away, and out of the country, over a lengthy period of time. Construction of the hotel was preceded by several trips to Japan — the first had been made in 1905 — and he would spend four years in Tokyo to complete the project.

The building was to replace an older, outdated hotel of the same name; the new structure would announce Japan's entry into the modern world and facilitate Western contacts through appropriate accommodations. As is so often the case, the job came through the right connections astutely pursued. Wright's own version was that a delegation of Japanese, sent by the emperor, sought him out in Wisconsin after having traveled around the world looking for a suitable architect, instantly (and, one assumes, humbly) offering him the job. The dates he gives for this visit are off, but no matter; it's prime Wright mythology.

The contact that led directly to the commission was made in Chicago, in 1911, through Frederick W. Gookin, a banker and fellow collector of Japanese prints. Gookin was one of a group of influential Japanese art enthusiasts that included Ernest Fenollosa, the distinguished leader of the "Boston orientalists"; Fenollosa's collection became the basis of the Boston Museum of Fine Arts' superb Japanese galleries. Wright had already acquired an outstanding group of prints by such masters as Hiroshige and Hokusai, and would buy masses of these popular woodblocks of landscapes, courtesans, and scenes of everyday life called ukiyo-e during his stay in Japan. Considered too common and vulgar for Japanese collectors, they could be purchased cheaply; his collection eventually numbered in the thousands.

Gookin knew Aisaku Hayashi, the manager of the existing Imperial Hotel. Gookin's recommendation of Wright was followed by a trip to Tokyo, with Mamah, in 1913, during which the matter was discussed. The project had been interrupted by the death of the Japanese emperor in 1912, and then resumed. Japan entered World War I on the side of the Allies in August 1914, and the United States followed in 1917. Wright worked on the commission all during the war years. The project became official in 1916, when Hayashi visited Taliesin and authorized Wright to continue with the design. Wright went to Tokyo again in 1917, where he developed plans and working drawings. At the end of October 1918, he sailed with Miriam and his son John, who would assist him, for an extended stay. Construction began in the summer of 1919. There were yearly voyages back to the States, but it is uncertain how many crossings he actually made; the boat took two weeks, and Wright was seasick all the way — it was a wretched trip for him each time. The day when architects would jet around the world, with instant electronic communications, was still a half century away. He did not return home for good until 1922.

The fame of the Imperial Hotel rests largely on the fact that it withstood the worst earthquake in Japan's history, the great Kanto earthquake of September 1, 1923, which killed more than 100,000 people and destroyed most of Tokyo.

Legend has it that the first news to reach America listing the "Imperial" structures that had been lost was interpreted by a Chicago paper, not surprised to find Wright a continuing, reliable source of catastrophic news, to include the Imperial Hotel. With communications cut off completely, it was days later that Wright received the famously worded telegram, "hotel stands undamaged as monument of your genius," signed by Baron Okura, the leader of the governmental and industrial consortium that had backed the project. Saved by its vaunted floating foundations, meant to move with the soft mud beneath them rather than breaking up, and Wright's insistence on including water as both a design and a fire safety feature, the hotel withstood the earthquake and the raging fire that followed. Hundreds of homeless were sheltered there.

Critics have considered the building a curious, transitional structure; it has been dismissed by many as odd and *retardataire*. Revisionist scholars, no longer bound by the rules of orthodox modernism, which it flouted in almost every way, have approached it differently; creating a "modern" building in Japan at that time, with the assurance that it would stand when the inevitable earthquake struck, was an enormous challenge. It required confidence of gargantuan proportions, which Wright never lacked, but it also needed a sure grasp of technology and an expert knowledge of local conditions; Wright brought his engineer, Paul Mueller, with him to Japan. The realization of an elaborate, unprecedented design and experimental engineering was an undertaking of great duration and difficulty that spanned almost a dozen years. As Arthur Drexler noted later in an exhibition of Wright drawings at the Museum of Modern Art, Wright had "the capacity to nourish inspiration with hard work." In addition, there were formidable obstacles of language and culture; he could work with his clients only through interpreters, and he found the conventions of Japanese communication maddeningly oblique. He was still emotionally exhausted and felt terribly alone.

The Japan he knew and described in the *Autobiography* is the old Japan, alien and beautiful, an exotic place of strangeness, character, and color. Wright was intensely visual, and his word pictures of Tokyo and its traditional customs and bustling activity are vividly evocative, a collage of sights and sounds. "Wide, bare-earth streets swarming with humanity . . . shuttered sedan chairs, scarlet and gold . . . the sound made by innumerable *geta* in the graveled streets . . . shops crammed with curious or brilliant merchandise . . . red paper lanterns on bamboo poles . . . little cages of fireflies . . . moon-lanterns glowing under spreading pine trees . . . *samisen* notes come from all directions like pervasive insect notes in a summer field . . . geisha . . . undulating noiselessly . . . Shunsho and Shigemasa's 'Beauties of the Little Green Houses . . .' it all looks . . . *just like the prints!*"

The Imperial Hotel rose slowly, out of confusion and chaos. Wright soon found that everything he had previously designed had to be redesigned on-site. He failed in his attempts to introduce modern methods of construction, fighting a losing battle with tradition, unable even to effect a compromise. The work was done painstakingly, by hand, on delicate bamboo scaffolding. There were problems with money and a governing board influenced by rumors and doubts about his design. Confidence was not restored until the building was almost complete in 1922, when it stood firm during a minor earthquake, much to Wright's relief. He was despairing and fearful of dismissal, almost to the end.

The staff he set up was an East-West mix. It included the European modernists Rudolf Schindler, who later established himself in California, and Antonin Raymond, who remained in Japan (both had been attracted by Wright's work and reputation), and the Japanese assistants and workmen who guided him through administrative and structural crises. He was allowed to create an apartment for himself in an annex of the hotel that he built quickly in 1919 after another existing annex burned. Serviced by the hotel, his living and working quarters consisted of a living room with a fireplace, a dining room, bedroom, and bath. A stair led to a rooftop studio and bedroom for his use when he worked late into the night. Balconies overlooked a garden. He records that there was also a "small" grand piano, found "not easily" somewhere in Tokyo.

In his impressive study *The Architecture of Frank Lloyd Wright*, Neil Levine described the Imperial Hotel as "a dour and ominously solemn mass of brick and lava stone." It was a building of enormous, ornamental complexity that neither mimicked Japanese style nor repeated Wright's previous work. Wright himself called it a battleship. He knew that he was "building against doomsday," as he later put it; he became totally preoccupied with the "terror of the temblor," completely possessed by the ageless threat and timeless imagery of Mt. Fuji. The sacred mountain became as central to the concept of his design as it was to the life and culture of Japan.

The building's battered walls of brick and concrete double shell construction, thicker at the bottom than at the top, rose at an angle to keep the center of gravity low. Long, low wings containing Western-style rooms surrounded a higher, central pavilion for social and official functions, with gardens and pools between. The structure was divided into sections, cantilevered, and jointed to avoid the rigidity that would rupture it under stress; the sections were individually attached to the floating base that was designed to move freely with the shocks. Pyramidal roofs ascended in overlapping planes, covered in greenish copper instead of the traditional tiles that became deadly flying missiles when an earthquake struck. The symbolism of Fuji, so constantly with him, was expressed in the rise of the hovering roofs over the lower wings, and in the substance of the soft, greenish, volcanic Oya stone that he chose for construction.

The reality of Wright's achievement is staggering. It was not that he invented anything — there are echoes of the Prairie house on a much larger scale — or that his building, alone, survived the earthquake intact. Both claims are easily disputed. But his vision was as original as it was practical. Characteristically, he had absorbed, adapted, and synthesized from many sources to create something that was uniquely his own but could still be read as an act of profound cultural respect. The excellence of the plan has long been acknowledged. To separate myth from reality, again, the "genius" saluted by Baron Okura must be credited in part to Wright's expert engineer, his old friend and working companion, Paul Mueller. Both were thoroughly familiar with the foundations used in Chicago for skyscraper construction on unstable soil. Wright's floating foundations were similar to earlier solutions developed in Tokyo in the 1890s, and those buildings sustained minimal damage. The ultimate reality is that the Imperial Hotel was an awesome accomplishment against formidable odds.

Impressive as the building must have

been, however, one suspects that it was not particularly cheerful or inviting. Statues of warriors guarded its portals. In photographs, its elaborately detailed Oya stone is overwhelming. The soaring and grottolike spaces covered with labyrinthine lava carvings of stylized peacocks and complex geometrical patterns are almost fantastically macabre. It could have been a wonderland or chamber of horrors; perhaps it was a bit of both. By the end of its life cycle as a hotel, the building seemed excessively gloomy to many, although it has become a cult object for some; its ornate exoticism had deteriorated badly and it was demolished in 1968. The building had outlived its time, but not its significance. Almost a decade later, the entrance and lobby were reerected in an outdoor museum of the Meiji period. For Wright, as Neil Levine noted perceptively, "the construction of the Imperial Hotel [was] evidence of his own ability to survive catastrophe . . . the mythical phoenix rising from the ashes."

But the job had taken its toll. Toward the end, he was constantly ill with the gastrointestinal complaint that afflicted many foreigners, and his mother, now eighty, took the arduous trip to Japan to be with him. Anna was treated reverently and royally by the Japanese, but her presence infuriated Miriam, who had relished her role at Wright's side as Madame Noel. All that remained to be completed was a duplicate wing of the building, which could be constructed without him. Unwell and fatigued, but by his own account triumphant, it was time for "Wright-san," as he referred to himself, to depart.

8

Like most architects, who exist from one project to the next, Wright lived in fear of being without work, even when involved in a major commission. He had already begun studies of the Imperial Hotel, but had yet to sign a contract, when he was introduced to Aline Barnsdall, an oil heiress and patron of the performing arts who had studied acting with Eleonora Duse in Europe and wanted to build a small theater in Chicago. From the time of their meeting, about a year after the tragedy at Taliesin, until the work was completed in 1921, the commission grew from a theater to a house surrounded by an arts complex, with artists' studios and residences as well as two theaters, for performance and films, and the venue had changed from Chicago to Los Angeles. The ambitious scheme was never completed, but it produced a remarkable house that signaled a radical change in Wright's style.

Hollyhock House, as Aline Barnsdall named it, after the hollyhocks that grew wild on the site and which she proclaimed were her favorite flower, was unlike anything Wright had designed or built before, or that even existed at the time. He approached the assignment as both a programmatic and a stylistic challenge. The site, Olive Hill, was a legendary location overlooking the surrounding Southern California hills, with views of the city and the ocean. A series of roof terraces command a spectacular outlook that could also be used for performances. But where Taliesin opened out to a verdant landscape, Hollyhock House was built around a central courtyard and pool; water moved through and around the building and the landscape as an integral part of the scheme. The entrance was through a templelike block with a frieze of stylized hollyhocks. In no established or identifiable style, the house bears the marks of many; the influences have been variously described as Aztec, Mayan, Egyptian, and Mexican pre-Columbian. If the look was archaic and vaguely Mesoamerican, the symmetrical plan and flanking wings still had a Beaux Arts formality.

The large living room, a classic double cube, was warmed by the golds and browns of Wright's furnishings and a magnificent gold-ground Japanese screen. The room focused on the hearth, but this one differed radically from those in Wright's earlier houses. Built of concrete block rather than brick, and embellished with abstract designs, it projected out into the room, occupying its own space. Instead of drawing one deeply into a shadowed, embracing isolation, it was placed beneath a skylight, with light flooding down from above. Even more unusual, it was set into a shallow pool of water at its base. Like some ceremonial symbol for the life of the house, it suggested life itself; all of the elements were there — fire, water, earth, and air.

When the industrial and scenic designer Norman Bel Geddes, who had been hired by Barnsdall for her theater project, saw early sketches of the house, he found it startling and enchanting; he called it "a miniature palace of some ancient civilization"; Wright called it "simply Californian." In a sense, he was right. It was an invention, and Southern California in the early 1920s was inventing itself. The movie industry, only recently arrived, was an exhilarating exercise in the glamorously unreal; Hollywood was a state of mind, a fantasy. Wright saw himself devising an indigenous architecture where none existed, creating a fairy-tale identity for a land that had been settled by strangers and their imports from home. Although the land soon became prime real estate, much of it was still wildly, profligately beautiful. Agnes de Mille has recorded her childhood memories of running through endless fields of brilliant flowers, when her uncle, Cecil B. De Mille, was making his epic films.

The sets for those films — Babylonian, Roman, Middle Eastern — were also part of the landscape. They were left standing where they were constructed, coexisting with the poppies and eucalyptus. Illusion defined perception and set the terms of occupation. Stars and studio heads built mansions in appropriated styles from French chateaux and English manor houses to Spanish colonial haciendas; the promised land was becoming a never-never land of architectural make-believe. Wright condemned it all as derivative and artificial — an architecture of default. He believed that a new, more suitable architecture was needed, and that he, of course, would create it; the style would be American, and identifiably his own. Unlike his counterparts in Europe, however, who rejected the past, he was not above seeking ideas in history and geography, although he would never acknowledge the sources of the forms and conventions that he used.

Ancient and primitive cultures had intrigued him since he had observed their influence on contemporary European art while he was abroad in 1909. He had seen exhibits of pre-Columbian cities and temples in Mexico and Central and South America as early as 1893, at the Chicago world's fair, and more recently, in models and photographs of Uxmal and Chichén Itzá displayed prominently at the Panama-Pacific Exposition of 1915 in California. He owned a set of photographs of the exhibits. Whatever his protestations to the contrary, he was an admirer and student of the great buildings of history, as all architects are; he never failed to add the new, the different, and the remote to his store of references. He considered the buildings of these early American civilizations, with their bold, monolithic forms and intrinsic decoration, closer geographically and culturally to California's lush landscape and benign climate than traditional styles imported from Europe or the East Coast. What he made of his sources of inspiration was pure invention, like everything else. If the implied regionalism was wishful rationalization, it provided an intriguing aesthetic potential for him to explore.

He gave his invention a name, California Romanza. In music, he explained, *romanza* was "free form, or freedom to make one's own" — something that seemed a perfect fit for the time and the place. Hollyhock House was also the stuff of dreams. The construction, which only looked like solid stone or concrete, was plaster over lath. Wright's romanticism was totally at odds with the austere anti-aesthetic minimalism that was gaining ground in Europe. The *romanza* of Hollyhock House, and the rationalism of Le Corbusier's Villa Savoye, a decade later, were at polemically opposite poles of modernism, although they eventually shared the same page of history.

Wright tells the story of the house with the wit and charming *mea culpa* that kept the faithful coming back for more outrageous behavior and extraordinary buildings. He was, he admitted, more interested in his creation than in the client, an apology tinged with after all, how could it be otherwise? He had been concerned with his own needs, his own search for expression, rather than her feelings and requirements — guilt admitted, therefore absolved. The house was built "by proxy," as he put it, while he was in Japan; construction had to be entrusted to others, and there were problems of design and execution. With John on the Tokyo project, supervision was delegated to his son Lloyd and an associate, Rudolf Schindler, and he blamed them for everything that went wrong or displeased him, listing their deficiencies with cruel precision. But much was Wright's own fault and he knew it. He was accustomed to resolving the practical details of his designs during construction, and he had not been there when he was needed. Faced with an unconventional building and an absentee architect, the contractor complained of a lack of working drawings, and followed the common practice of urging compromises on the client. The client, in turn, was constantly advised by her "entourage of friends," as Wright described them in half-humorous accusations, who knew about as much about the building, he said, "as Sodom knew of Sanctity." Absorbed in the construction of the Imperial Hotel, "in utter weariness," he had abdicated control.

To make things more difficult, the architect's and the client's egos were a strong-willed match. Mercurial and self-absorbed, used to doing as they pleased and getting what they wanted, his willful, wealthy, women clients were not easy to deal with. He found Aline Barnsdall particularly troublesome; she was given to running off to distant parts of the globe to "refresh" herself whenever decision making threatened. Her architect was equally free-floating; when she was in California he was in Japan, when he came back, she was gone. En route, "she would drop suggestions as a war-plane drops bombs and sail away into the blue." He wondered what she needed a house for, since she was "as domestic as a shooting star." He wrote in retrospect, "Though both architect and client were torn to tatters, 'Form' got into the building despite all folly." It was the "idea" of the house that mattered to him, "the thing of beauty" that he tried to nurture from afar, and that, "miraculously," he said, was finally achieved.

Aline Barnsdall did not stay long in Hollyhock House; she seldom alighted anywhere for any length of time. With ideas of "democratizing" art, and her association with such bona fide radicals of the day as Emma Goldman, she was considered a "parlor Bolshevik" in Hollywood. The divide was exacerbated by the fact that she lived grandly, cut off from the city and its inhabitants in elegant, artful, and extravagant architectural seclusion on the hill.

To Wright's consternation, she suddenly "gave it all away," donating the house and land to the city of Los Angeles, which dithered about accepting it until 1927, and did so finally through an arrangement with a California arts group, which had neither the means nor the expertise to deal with the building. Treated with minimal appreciation and casual conservation, the house deteriorated badly. Municipal caretakers added the ultimate insult of a chain-link fence. The private-public coalition that finally undertook its restoration and maintenance after many years of neglect struggled with a chronic lack of funds.

When Wright returned from Japan in July 1922, he failed to find the remembered comforts and pleasures at Taliesin. There had been many changes in his absence. Chicago was no longer a center of experimental activity; the creative energy was gone and conservative tastes ruled in the East and Midwest. His contacts had been broken, and the clients who had so eagerly sought him out were things of the past. Miriam's agitation and symptoms seemed to increase. Just three months after

Catherine finally agreed to a divorce, Anna Wright died, in February 1923.

He had confidently expected to find himself famous and besieged by commercial and institutional clients with the completion and dramatic survival of the Imperial Hotel, but he discovered that he had been essentially forgotten, as frequently happens to architects who spend a long time abroad. The four years in Japan had isolated him from everything happening at home. Although he never ceased to make the claim that he was modernism's sole inventor, he would be relegated to the twilight of its beginnings by champions of the International style, which moved from Europe to the intellectual avant-garde in the United States in the 1930s. Wright was never a doctrinaire modernist. He committed the original architectural sin of conforming to no ideology except his own, and the equally unforgivable sin to defenders of modernist dogma of changing styles whenever he wanted to.

However, a year after his return, Wright was referring to the stylistic extravagance of both the Imperial Hotel and Hollyhock House as an "indulgence"; he had strayed far from his own avant-garde principles in following an aberrant, picturesque path.

He had endorsed the machine as early as his Hull House lecture of 1901, and he now felt conscience-bound to return to the progressive ideal of standardized construction. That reawakening was perhaps due to the increasing competition of the machine-art modernists; as much as he derided them, they had the constructive effect of making him reexamine his own direction. But he did it in his own way, and in his own fashion. His immediate response was to abandon the plaster Romanza of Hollyhock House for an innovative system of prefabricated "textile block" houses. But his more lasting contribution was the small, reproducible Usonian house of the 1930s, which became synonymous with his name.

If any part of the country provided the climate for something new, it was California, then, as now, the perpetual land of opportunity and change. His son Lloyd had moved to Los Angeles in 1910 to work with Irving Gill on a series of modernist houses in the European style, and had stayed on. Wright saw the West Coast as the last architectural frontier and, following the completion of Hollyhock House, he opened an office in Los Angeles, in 1923. With Lloyd's help, he built a series of the textile block houses in California in the 1920s. Japan had been a refuge after Mamah's death, and California was another escape from the memories of Taliesin. Essentially, he was starting over.

He now turned to the commonest of mass-produced materials, the concrete block, which he believed could be standardized in design and production for a quick, easy, affordable, and handsome way of building. He would transform this ugly duckling into a prefabricated swan. The blocks would be cast in molds with his own abstract and stylized patterns, and held together by steel reinforcing rods. They would then be erected as a double wall made rigid with concrete. The surface patterns ranged from abstract geometric motifs to stylized flower forms; the blocks could suggest a solid mass, or be used as exotically pierced screens. The space between the inner and outer walls provided insulation. Wright called the method "weaving," and the concrete and steel units were to substitute for a many-layered process of putting multiple materials together with time-consuming labor. He saw the standardized, partially prefabricated system as something that could be used by unskilled labor, at minimum cost. The idea was radical and the effect, not surprisingly, looked a lot like California Romanza. He had it both ways.

As with many inventions, the reasoning was unassailable and the execution problematic; the dream of mass production with cheap labor turned into the reality of overestimated efficiencies, with handwork, delays, and cost overruns, when unskilled workers required modifications of the process. But the textile block houses built for Charles Ennis, Samuel Freeman, Alice Millard, and John Storer between 1923 and 1925 are boldly original, and unforgettable in their settings. The Ennis house is powerful and idiosyncratic, standing like a fortress on a steep hill. It has successfully resisted the efforts of subsequent owners to turn it into something pretentiously baronial by adding marble and massive chandeliers. Those who fight Wright, even in absentia, usually lose. The Freeman house, with a less weighty, more open block design, is modest, mysterious, and enchanting. Wright's low, shadowed entrance leads to a sudden release into light and space, as in the Playroom at Oak Park. A large living room has corner windows of invisibly joined glass, a radical feature then, opening to the view of an unexpected, enveloping landscape. The house seems to cascade down the hillside, almost swallowed by lush vegetation.

One house is a masterpiece — a flawed masterpiece, but a marvel nevertheless; a defective but indisputable beauty. La Miniatura — the name Wright gave it for its small size and suggestive Hispano-Moresque aura — was built for a client of enduring, heroic patience, Alice Millard, a widow and collector of books, art, and antiques. If Aline Barnsdall was an absentee devil, Alice Millard was an ever present angel, a true believer who tolerated all the trials and tribulations her house and architect provided, which were almost biblical in their nonstop intensity.

Wright rejected the original site for "a beautiful little ravine" with two eucalyptus trees, in which the house sat like a jewel. The look of the sand-colored, pierced, textured block was surprisingly monumental, although the building was intimate in scale. But here the blocks had no steel reinforcing rods; they were held together with mortar. The project was plagued from the start by construction problems, dampness, and leaks. Delays were endemic and costs soared. Immediately after completion, torrential rains coursed down the ravine and created waterfalls, inside and out. Wright's leaking roofs are not myths, and the stories are an endless delight to those snug under the tight roofs of their suburban split-levels or McMansions, where there is little taste for gambling with Romanza. Built before the development of silicone seals and rubber roofing products, Wright's houses relied on what was available, and the existing technology often failed to match what he envisioned. The fault, he told Mrs. Millard, was that of the contractor, who had failed to carry out his specifications. The fault also could have been the architect's, who failed to check what was being done. The cavalier contractor had followed a disappearing contractor, who evaporated with prepaid funds given by a trusting Mrs. Millard before she left on a trip to Europe; when finally located, he was using the money to build an elaborate place of his own. Wright heard about the leaks belatedly, from his uncomplaining client, and claimed to have made the necessary corrections.

Leaks, delays, and costs were to become facts of life for Wright's clients. There were no off-the-shelf products, no standardized procedures, for his unconventional buildings. His preliminary designs, while conceptually complete, were essentially schematics to be fully developed as the work progressed; the problems that arose were resolved during construction. There were always problems, and he could always solve them. But as any experienced client or contractor knows, there is no more expensive way to build than this ad hoc, custom procedure with its booby-trapped "extras"; it is simply not possible to calculate final costs or hold to a firm budget. By talent, temperament, and the way he worked, Wright virtually guaranteed the overruns. Whatever it took in time or money for the right solution or proper finish was justified in his mind, just as the quality of his life justified the cost of maintaining it. The ideas were often elegantly simple and rational; it was in the execution that costs and complications ensued.

Wright was not only an innovator, he was a hands-on builder — one of the last of the master builders, in the great tradition of the art. He dictated every detail, including how the houses should be lived in, and clients would complain as much about the tyranny of his control as the unpredictability of the expense. It took a giant leap of faith to deal with the trials and terrors of unprecedented ideas and unproved technology. Some found it a transformational, life-enhancing experience.

In November 1923, as soon as the legally required waiting time after his divorce from Catherine was up, Wright married Miriam Noel. The ceremony took place at Taliesin, in the middle of a bridge over the Wisconsin River, at midnight. The romanticism of the event did nothing to improve the relationship. One wonders why, after so much misery, Wright made this commitment. He usually took the road of least resistance with his strong-willed women. But it is tempting to believe, in spite of his reputation for bad behavior, that he was a gentleman of a certain generation, and only a gentleman feels guilt. He knew he had caused her pain, and he believed he owed her this after all they had done to each other. No matter how often he defended free and open relationships he understood, as a man of his time, that a woman sacrificed her reputation and place in society by cohabiting without marriage, and that he, the man, was the agent of ostracism. He acknowledged as much in the *Autobiography*. How different the story would have been fifty years later! How irrelevant and unremarkable it all would have seemed after women's liberation and the sexual revolution made "living in sin" an archaic oddity. He also thought that marriage might "calm" her; in fact, her condition deteriorated after the wedding. Guilt had undoubtedly been a factor in a visit he made to a psychiatrist looking for a clinical explanation for her irrational and punishing behavior to absolve him of his emotional ambivalence. The advice he said he was given, to let her go for her own good, to "save" her from her own destructive impulses, must have justified his relief when she left Taliesin, ending the marriage just a few months later.

He was not without feminine companionship for long. Soon after Miriam's departure, he met Olga Lazovich Hinzenberg, an attractive young woman from a distinguished Montenegrin family, whose artistic and mystical inclinations appealed to him instantly. They were both attending a ballet performance in Chicago, where she had come from Paris to discuss business matters with her estranged husband, Vlademar Hinzenberg, a Russian architect who had emigrated to America. She was twenty-six, Wright was fifty-seven. Her youth, her dark eyes and dark hair drawn back simply from her face, her vaguely ethnic way of dressing, beyond fashion, were all in marked contrast to Miriam's costumed drama. She had left her husband after the war, and gone to Paris with her young daughter, Svetlana, where she became a follower of Georgi Gurdjieff, the charismatic leader of a spiritual lifestyle taught at his Institute for the Harmonious Development of Man. Olgivanna, as Wright always called her, had spent several years with Gurdjieff, in Paris and Fontainebleau, the group's headquarters, as a student and teacher. The physical and spiritual hardships of a demanding regime of philosophy, mysticism, music, poetry, exercise, and dance, combined with hard work, fasting, and very little sleep, had equipped her well for the stresses of her future life with Wright. In a few months, by the spring of 1925, she had moved in with him. Shortly after her arrival at Taliesin, she divorced her husband.

Wright was beginning to recover his practice and prestige. There was enough work to take on draftsmen, and the young Europeans who continued to flock to his studio for the privilege of working with him included the Austrian architect Richard Neutra, who later made an independent reputation for sleek modernist houses in California. A variety of projects was on the boards: a skyscraper for an insurance company in Chicago, a country club in Madison, and an early version of the spiral that always fascinated and preoccupied him — an Automobile Objective and Planetarium meant as a destination when people still took pastoral Sunday drives. This spiral theme would be realized as New York's Guggenheim Museum, thirty years later.

His work abroad was appearing in important publications in Germany and the Netherlands; he was featured in the Dutch avant-garde magazine *Wendingen,* and the articles became an impressive monograph, *The Life-Work of the American Architect Frank Lloyd Wright,* by the Dutch architect H. Th. Wijdeveld. The future looked bright. And then it all began to fall apart. In April 1925, there was a second fire at Taliesin. The cause, this time, was defective wiring. The living area was again completely destroyed, and many of the old and rare treasures acquired during his trips to Japan — those irresistible works of art he bought with his fees instead of paying bills — were lost in the flames. To get the money he needed to rebuild, Wright was forced to mortgage everything he owned: house, studio, land, livestock, and all of his possessions. The new debt was piled on the still unpaid debt for the first rebuilding, after the fire of 1914.

In July, more than a year after Miriam's departure, he sued for divorce on the grounds of desertion. The proceedings went quietly until Miriam learned of Olgivanna's presence at Taliesin. Enraged when she discovered that Olgivanna was pregnant with Wright's child — a daughter, Iovanna, was born in December 1925 — she began a campaign of bitter and violent harassment. She tried to have Olgivanna deported as an alien, forcing her to leave the hospital, exhausted and ill, immediately after the delivery. During one of her madder moments, after obtaining a warrant for Wright's arrest, she broke into Taliesin, claiming it as her home, destroying whatever she could before being forcibly removed. She countersued for divorce claiming physical cruelty. In August 1926, she sued Olgivanna for alienation of affection and an astronomical $100,000; the suit was eventually dismissed.

Late that summer, under the stress of Miriam's escalating legal threats and mounting problems at Taliesin, Wright was advised by his lawyer to go away until his marital troubles could be resolved and things settled down. He fled secretly with Olgivanna and the two children — Svetlana and the infant Iovanna — to a hideaway in a lakeside cottage in Minnesota, but rather than finding quiet anonymity there, the couple's "disappearance" with their "love child" ignited the press. The story had everything — illicit sex, an out-of-wedlock baby, a vengeful "outraged" wife, suits and countersuits, and deep trouble with money and the law. Miriam obligingly provided copious copy. Splashy headlines identified the missing couple as "fugitives from justice." Olgivanna was referred to as a "Montenegrin dancer." By this time, Miriam and Olgivanna's ex-husband shared the same lawyer (a match, one suspects, made by Miriam in her wild pursuit of vengeance); Hinzenberg now claimed that his daughter Svetlana had been "abducted" and began action to obtain custody, on the grounds that Olgivanna was a morally unfit mother. He also sued Wright for alienation of affection.

It defies belief that Wright could make the same mistake twice — having taken the unwed Olgivanna from Wisconsin to the Minnesota hideout, he was once again accused of illegally transporting a woman across state lines for immoral purposes. They were discovered after two months, in late October, and arrested on charges of adultery and violation of the Mann Act. Wright, Olgivanna, the nursing infant, and the young Svetlana were all carried off to Hennepin County jail, where they spent two nights, behind clanging gates in separate cells, with an assortment of not unfriendly criminals. By the second night, Wright was established as a celebrity among the prisoners; in recognition of his status, the warden replaced his soiled mattress and had his cell cleaned. The next day he succeeded in reaching a lawyer and obtaining bail. On his release, he offered to buy his fellow inmates a dinner of pork chops and mashed potatoes, but there is no record of whether they received it. Later, the Mann Act charges were dropped, and Olgivanna and Hinzenberg reached an agreement on joint custody of Svetlana. But Wright's notoriety had peaked. When he tried to obtain life insurance, he was refused because of too much publicity.

Then things really bottomed out. He had not been able to meet his mortgage payments on Taliesin, and in September 1926, while he was still in hiding, the Bank of Wisconsin announced its intention to foreclose. With no choice, and at the bank's insistence, he was forced to sell his Japanese print collection at auction. His most valuable prints went to a gallery in New York, where they were sold for far less than they were worth, with the gallery taking a usurious 35 percent fee. Declaring herself co-owner of Wright's assets, Miriam tried to claim the money, but the bank attached the funds; still, the amount fell far short of the sum needed for his debt.

Playing the heavy, the Bank of Wisconsin would not allow Wright to remain at Taliesin until full payment was made. The bank had already arranged to take over the maintenance staff, and he was formally evicted. Wright, Olgivanna, and the children were, literally, homeless. They spent the winter of 1926 in a rented beach house in La Jolla, California, where Miriam followed them, once again invading the house and smashing everything she could reach. Whatever Olgivanna's endurance training with Gurdjieff, she had never fully recovered from the birth of Iovanna, and she now grew weak and thin. In the spring of 1927, they went to New York to fight the deportation charges. The Bank of Wisconsin had already sold all the Taliesin livestock, and was preparing to auction everything else. In May, Wright's new lawyer, Philip La Follette, a future governor of Wisconsin, arranged for a year's grace from the bank, which allowed Wright to go back to Taliesin to work. But the bank, in an act worthy of some Victorian melodrama, stipulated that he was not permitted to live there "illegally" with Olgivanna, since they were not married. The bank could not condone, or finance, sin.

The divorce from Miriam finally came through in August 1927 — by now it was obvious to all that she was deranged — but under Wisconsin law Wright would still have to wait a year to marry. La Follette and Wright's friends took care of Miriam's settlement and alimony, and La Follette suggested a year's discreet absence for Olgivanna, until the divorce was "absolute," while Wright resumed work at Taliesin. He refused. Because he was no closer to being able to pay off his debt than ever, an idea born in desperation — whether it was one of Wright's wilier schemes or a brainchild of his lawyer is uncertain — was now put into action. To protect him and his earnings from lawsuits and creditors, and with the hope of imposing some order and control on his affairs, his friends incorporated him as Frank Lloyd Wright, Inc. Probably knowing it was a terrible investment, but always optimistic, friends, clients, and family bought shares. The ever willing Darwin Martin contributed generously; the motley group of other shareholders included the playwright Charles MacArthur, the critic Alexander Woollcott, and Wright's sister Maginel. It was a valiant effort, but they were never able to unsnarl Wright's tangled finances. Needing to reach the awful Miriam at one point during the divorce negotiations, his benefactors asked where she was, and he had no idea. "Only Frank would be careless enough to misplace a wife," a bemused Darwin Martin reported to his equally patient brother.

Things could not have gotten worse, but they did. Discovering that Wright had returned to Taliesin with Olgivanna, the Bank of Wisconsin informed him that he could no longer live or work there because "the premises were being used for immoral purposes." The mortgage was "outraged," Wright reported. "The mortgage objecting, we were asked to leave." The family was homeless again. Salvation came from Albert Chase McArthur. A former Wright apprentice, young Albert McArthur was designing a new luxury hotel in Phoenix, the Arizona Biltmore, for his brothers, Charles and Warren Jr. Once again, in Wright's Rashomon-like life, there are two versions of the story; the reader is at liberty to decide which is true. Either the brothers, concerned about Albert's inexperience, asked Wright to help, or Albert himself wrote — this is Wright's account — to inquire about the possibility of using the textile block system of construction for the hotel. An excellent idea, Wright supposedly wrote back to Arthur, and he, Wright, would be happy to come to Arizona as a consultant, with his family, for an extended stay. A contract was signed requiring Wright's presence in Phoenix in early 1928. How much was consultation and how much was actual design has never been accurately determined; the drawings of the hotel were credited to McArthur. Under the circumstances, Wright maintained a professional anonymity, although he objected strongly to the insertion of conventional construction behind his concrete block system by doubting engineers, as well as the addition of a fourth floor. As a consultant, however, he lacked the authority to override the decision.

Meanwhile, back at Taliesin, the melodrama continued. The date passed for re-payment to the bank, which took over title to the land and buildings and announced an auction for the end of May 1928. The sale failed to attract bidders, and the bank bought the property back on the promise that the backers of Frank Lloyd Wright, Inc., would raise the money to acquire it. In August, the beleaguered couple was finally legally free to marry; the hand-colored wedding invitations had a picture of the two-and-a-half-year-old Iovanna at the top. The honeymoon was spent in Phoenix. In September, the corporation produced the necessary funds for the bank. In October, the newlyweds went home to Taliesin. A year later, in 1929, Miriam Noel fell ill and died. The worst period of Wright's perpetually troubled existence since the horrors of the 1914 tragedy came to an end. He had lost almost four years of his working life.

9

This was hardly an auspicious moment to restart a career. The boom of the 1920s came to a sudden and catastrophic end in October 1929, when the stock market crashed and the Great Depression began. Projects were dropped, buildings already started would stand unfinished for years, and one of Wright's most promising schemes, a luxury hotel, San Marcos-in-the-Desert — commissioned by an Arizona entrepreneur and pioneer, Dr. Alexander Chandler, who controlled a large tract of desert land — was aborted for lack of funds. Wright spent much of his time writing and lecturing and devising schemes for survival.

But the Arizona experience proved to be a turning point, an opening of options and sensibilities, in which serendipity, as usual, played a notable part. Chandler and Wright met in 1928, while Wright was working on the Arizona Biltmore. The two men seemed to have struck a sympathetic chord immediately. Chandler's holdings included a town named for himself, Chandler, Arizona, and the popular San Marcos Hotel located there, which he hoped to turn into an upscale rival to the Arizona Biltmore; he was looking for an architect when he heard that Wright was in Phoenix. Wright shared the older man's ambitious vision. He also shared Chandler's great love of the desert. He was awed and enchanted by its light and colors, the intense sun and endless sky, the rock formations and distant hills, the giant saguaros and the strangely flowering vegetation; he had fallen under its spell during earlier visits and the attachment to its awesome beauty grew stronger during the Biltmore consultancy. As Reyner Banham wrote in a brilliant article in the 1960s, the desert was a revelation and life-changing experience for Wright in many ways.

Wright began work on San Marcos-in-the-Desert in the spring of 1928, and he completed the designs during the enforced sojourn that summer with Olgivanna in La Jolla, when they were still forbidden to return to Taliesin. The drawings were shown to Chandler during the couple's honeymoon in Arizona after their marriage in September, and a contract was signed. The return to Wisconsin was finally permitted in October, but the contract with Chandler required Wright's presence in Arizona during construction, and in early January 1929, in a blinding blizzard, he moved home and office to Arizona, intending to stay for the duration of the job. Unable to find inexpensive lodging for the fifteen members of his entourage, which included apprentices, workmen, his family, and a nurse for the children, he constructed a temporary camp on Chandler's land near the Salt Range Mountains. The Ocatilla desert camp, which he named for the scarlet-flame flower of the ocotillo bush, was the precursor of Taliesin West, the camp he built later, near Scottsdale, where the entire Taliesin establishment moved from Wisconsin every year for the winter months.

Wright quickly drew up the camp plans in a cold, empty room of the Chandler town offices; he put the drawing boards on boxes and his apprentices handed him the tools. Construction started early the next day as the sun rose over "a sublime spectacle of desert mountain ranges and gorgeous sunrise sky." Exhilarated by the prospect and the setting, shivering and singing in the desert morning chill, he recalled that they ate breakfast "in that wonderful dining-room sixty miles wide, as long and tall as the universe."

They built fifteen cabins, canvas-roofed on wooden frames; connecting wood walls made an angular enclosure around a central campfire with raised seats. The red of the ocotillo flower was painted in the end panels. The camp was "like a group of gigantic butterflies with scarlet wing spots," he wrote, "conforming gracefully to the outcropping of black splintered rock gently uprising from the desert floor," or "some new kind of desert fleet . . . like ships coming down the mesa."

Through the desert prism, he saw things differently. "The white luminous canvas overhead . . . the diffusion of light within, was so enjoyable and sympathetic to the desert . . . that I felt oppressed by the thought of the opaque solid overhead of the much too heavy Midwestern houses. . . . Out here in the great spaces . . . the too obvious wearies the eye too soon, stultifies the imagination. Obvious symmetry closes the episode before it begins." The straight line and the flat plane, he said, must become "the dotted line, the broad, low, extended plane textured because in all of this astounding desert there is not one hard, undotted line to be seen." The lightness and strength, the asymmetry of the camp, suggested ways of building beyond symmetry, beyond the usual, beyond convention.

Once again, Wright was using nature — in both his response to the setting and the themes and motifs that he turned into evocative abstractions. The striated and notched façades that ran uninterrupted from top to bottom of the buildings he designed for San Marcos were his reworking of the saguaro cactus. "Every flat plane is grosgrained, patterned like the Saguaro itself," he said, "the entire building is an abstraction of this mountain region." The scheme carried his textile block system further, both structurally and aesthetically, than in the earlier California houses. Studies and mock-ups made on the site used the blocks for an integrated, overall pattern rather than as repeated, individual units. The buildings were to be terraced and stepped back, giving each room a balcony and wide-ranging views — a device that later became nearly universal for resort hotels. He would use the analogy of the saguaro again in his project for St. Mark's-in-the-Bouwerie in New York, an apartment tower that he described as having the same inner structure as the saguaro — "interior vertical rods [that] hold it rigidly upright, maintaining its great fluted columnar mass for centuries." He called it "a perfect example of reinforced building construction."

But San Marcos was not to be. When Chandler was unable to raise the money after the October stock market crash, the $40,000 fee that Wright had been counting on for financial deliverance evaporated with the project. Instead, he had to add a $19,000 deficit to his escalating Taliesin debt. He must have been an eternal optimist. Or his resolve was as steely as his ambition and his belief in his own gifts and mission. No project failed, no commission was lost, which he did not see as the seeds of some future achievement. Even ephemera like Ocatilla had lessons to teach, unique aspects to be understood. Within a season of the return to Taliesin, Ocatilla was gone, destroyed for its materials; "the Indians," he noted, "had carted it all away."

Reyner Banham has described Wright's trips to the desert and time spent there as his "wilderness years" — a period in which he endured both a professional wilderness and a wilderness of the spirit, of professional isolation, and of physical and emotional uprooting. "And the desert shook him," Banham wrote, "as it must shake anybody. Not only is it ravishingly and inhumanly beautiful, but it marks the situation where the accessibility of the wilderness becomes frankly disturbing. . . ." For an exile from Midwestern suburbia, whose travels had taken him to old civilizations in Europe and Asia, the desert was a powerful, inspirational, and liberating experience. What it generated, according to Banham, was a new freedom, a rejection of conventional planning — a "freedom from axial symmetry, from right angles, from centralized spaces," from the more traditional geometry that characterized his earlier work. He was on a trajectory to the lightness and utility of the Usonian house, and the flights of fancy embraced in his later years.

As the May heat began, and snakes and other winter-dormant creatures invaded the camp, Wright acquired a used Packard sport phaeton, "open to the sky," for the family's trip back to Wisconsin. The itinerary was circuitous and the ride must have seemed endless; he was notorious for the unpredictability of his routes. They went from Arizona to Chicago to New York, where he consulted on the St. Mark's

242

project, also doomed to remain unbuilt as the Depression deepened. By the late 1920s, Wright had developed an international persona and reputation, but these were fallow years, for him and the rest of the profession.

At the lowest point of his enforced inactivity, while in hiding from the law and creditors in the Minnesota lakeside bungalow with Olgivanna, he had begun his *Autobiography* at her urging. This extraordinary document, revised and republished twice at later dates, was a creative and cathartic exercise in selective memory and events that reveals as it conceals. Its truths and its lies are woven together in a narrative history and philosophical ruminations that swing from great descriptive beauty to long passages of moral and aesthetic preaching that try the reader's patience and comprehension cruelly. Modeled after the memoirs of Louis Sullivan and Henry Adams, and written in a Whitmanesque prose with bursts of a highly personal style, it has been dismissed by critics as a failed literary effort. But much of it is wonderful in its descriptive passages of places, landscape, and sites. This is Wright as he saw himself, and as he wanted to be seen. His own words, true or false, bring us closest to a complex, gifted, dedicated, egocentric, arrogant, deeply believing, self-deluding, willfully embattled man. What could only be conveyed in person, however, was the charisma and wit that tempered his calculated performance and accompanied his most outrageous actions and pronouncements.

The *Autobiography* was published in 1932, in the context of a world that was moving on to other intellectual and artistic fashions. It was not that Wright's genius was unrecognized, or that his work lacked respect, but that his achievements were considered part of the past. He was sixty-five, an age at which most men retired. Thirty years of producing innovative and celebrated buildings could be considered a full and finished career. He had demonstrated an endless capacity for change and development, but no one expected him to continue. A younger generation saw him as an eccentric, irascible old man whose "time had come and gone." In 1932, he was without work or prospects, but that was true for most of the profession. He had no money — no novelty for him — but neither did anyone else. He was expert at avoiding those to whom he owed substantial sums, convinced that they, not he, were at fault in their computations or untimely demands. He always believed that money would be found or come his way, and in the meantime he begged and bluffed, with insolence and charm, to maintain himself as he saw fit.

Without other means of support, and thrust into the role of elder statesman, he wrote and lectured widely. He had begun to receive the honors and invitations that he felt were long overdue. The Akademie der Kunst in Berlin made him an "extraordinary honorary member" in 1929. He gave the Kahn Lectures at Princeton University in 1930, which he published as *Modern Architecture* the following year. He and Olgivanna were the guests of the Pan American Union in Rio de Janeiro, where he judged a competition for a Columbus memorial. A retrospective exhibition of his work was held in New York in 1931 and then traveled abroad, to Amsterdam, Brussels, Frankfurt, and Berlin.

But 1932 was also the year he was consigned to history by New York's recently established and instantly influential Museum of Modern Art. The often irrational resentment that Wright had been harboring against the perceived injustices and betrayals of critics and colleagues deepened into hurt and anger when the museum mounted its now historic show, "Modern Architecture: International Exhibition," organized by a neophyte Philip Johnson, who would become a pivotal power player and tastemaker in the architectural world, and the young (and still unhyphenated) Henry-Russell Hitchcock, just beginning his career as a distinguished architectural historian. What was new, and modern, to both men and to the museum, was not Wright, but the European movement known from then on as the International style. The exhibition celebrated Le Corbusier, Walter Gropius, Mies van der Rohe, the German Bauhaus, the Dutch De Stijl, the Austrian Richard Neutra, and a few talented Americans working in the European style.

Because Wright's buildings did not fit into the narrowly dogmatic stylistic rules of a machine-art modernism defined by the show, the two curators, uncertain of what to do with his work, passed it over. Urged to stress something American if possible, they reconsidered; in the on-again, off-again negotiations that ensued, Wright initially refused to be part of the exhibition. "I find I don't speak the same language nor am I in step with its aims and purposes," he wrote Johnson in a letter in which personal insults and expressions of high principle compete for space. Admitting that he was known as a troublesome, uncompromising egotist, he declared that he might as well live up to his reputation, deriding the "cut-paper style" of the architects Johnson and Hitchcock had chosen, and berating them for "the taint of propaganda in the personal examples you prefer." He concluded, "I find myself a man without a country, architecturally speaking, at the present time," adding that he saw no reason to "join your procession and belie my own principles of architecture and conduct. . . . I shall at least not have sold out!"

Eventually, he was included in a section on housing, for which he belligerently prepared a "house on the mesa" meant to demonstrate his mastery of modernism by their definition and his own. Protesting and regretting his inclusion until the end of the show, he maintained an abrasive relationship with the museum, although it later mounted major displays of his work. Johnson, who continued to dismiss Wright as "the greatest architect of the nineteenth century," revised his assessment later on.

But the division between Wright and the

proponents and practitioners of the International style was real and deep, as Neil Levine has demonstrated. "To the geometric abstraction of International Style modernism," Levine writes, "Wright offered a highly figurative naturalism, to the Europeans' mechanistic functionalism, he countered with a romantic expressionism, to their . . . standardization, he proposed instead a material- and site-specific ad hocism, and to their collective vision of a regularized urban order, he opposed a pragmatic individualism based on typically American patterns of land use and development."

Wright never stopped stressing his dedication to the search for a truly American architecture, or claiming full credit for its invention. He saw his work as the embodiment of a profound truth of time and place, against the superficial and fashionable "homogenizing" mannerisms of the European modernism being embraced by the cultural elite. His ideal of an organic architecture in which nature and building were one, his emphasis on site, materials, and evocative details, the symbolism with which he infused his forms, his warmer and more easily understood domesticity, all made his buildings seem old-fashioned next to the stark white surfaces and sleek machine-art style of his rivals. He was called a traditionalist, and even worse, a "new traditionalist," a term that acknowledged his innovations but made them, and him, part of history. He perpetuated the split, never missing an opportunity to deride the "antiseptic, operating room" look of his European "enemies." But his real feelings must have been mixed, because he knew talent when he saw it. He admired Richard Neutra's Lovell house in Los Angeles before the two men became open enemies. As he had always responded to every kind of stimulus in the past, he continued to study, absorb, and incorporate anything that interested him and was relevant to his own constantly evolving style.

He was, of course, not about to accept the museum's evaluation. He was four years into a new marriage and the father of a young child, and more confident than ever that he could design important new buildings. He was a tireless worker who could wear out younger men. And he was a notorious survivor. His life had been a battle against tragedy, adversity, and his own intransigence. He would fight harder than ever to maintain the position he felt entitled to as artist and innovator.

A skilled and opportunistic manipulator of publicity and the press, he went on the attack, in person and in print. He chastised cultural and intellectual leaders continually for their sins, which consisted chiefly of not recognizing him as the sole representative of architectural truth, and attacked the profession for its blindness to the exclusive validity of organic architecture. As his sense of injustice and paranoia increased, his enemies list, which ranged from the Beaux Arts to the Bauhaus, grew to include the American Institute of Architects and, on a more personal level, all contractors, lawyers, real estate agents, bankers, and clients' wives. His tart, controversial, and intensely personal opinions were a constant source of copy for the press. Mere ignorance never stopped him; he would pontificate on any subject shamelessly, whether he knew anything about it or not.

He relished the publicity, even when his cavalier treatment of facts diminished the seriousness of his public persona. As Reyner Banham observed, "he relied on his personal charm and charisma, much more than on logic and information." To ensure the attention he believed he deserved, he persistently proclaimed himself to be America's greatest architect, and then, more shamelessly, the greatest architect in the world, and finally, the greatest architect of all time. How much of this he actually believed — and one suspects he believed most or all of it and certainly found it useful to provoke attention, argument, and response — he had an unwavering faith in his talent and his convictions and was capable of dedication and deviousness in their service. But his semimystical union of craft and spirit in the romantic nineteenth-century tradition of Emerson and Ruskin found no sympathetic response from a new generation for whom the great Victorians no longer had meaning or significance, and who failed to understand how radical Wright's innovations had been, and continued to be. He was considered passé by the champions of functionalism who drew inspiration from industry and technology rather than from nature. He was outside of the cultural moment, and its repercussions in art and society.

Unable to raise funds from his usual loyal rescuers — his greatest patron and easiest touch, Darwin Martin, died in 1935, foreclosing much future support — but never at a loss for schemes to stay afloat, he decided to become an educator rather than an employer. There were, of course, neither commissions nor employees at this time. He had always relied on the talented young men and women who flocked to the studio to work for him; now he would replace employees with apprentices, who would "learn by doing." Instead of paying them, they would pay him for the privilege. And so, in 1932, out of ingenuity and desperation, a brilliant scheme was formed to turn penury into profit, or at least keep Taliesin functioning. Aided by Olgivanna's experience as a former Gurdjieff disciple and teacher, the Taliesin Fellowship was born.

As always with Wright, the Fellowship in concept was far grander than it would be in reality; practical considerations quickly reduced its size and scope. The ambitious prospectus he wrote and sent out called for seventy apprentices who would pay $650 each for a yearlong experience as part of a commune that would include living quarters, meals, interaction with distinguished residents in dance, pottery, weaving, and other artistic pursuits, and whatever architectural knowledge could be gleaned from proximity to the great man. The Fellowship would be physically and financially self-supporting. The text described a cooperative, self-sufficient community, with four hours of each day — two in the morning, and two in the afternoon — spent doing farmwork and domestic chores; the rest of the day would be devoted to artistic and intellectual pursuits. The apprentices would grow their own food and build their own quarters; the "hands-on" construction of residences and studios would be "learning by doing." In the evening, there would be entertainment — concerts by those who had musical talents, with guest performances and lectures. Wright emphasized that there would be no conventional instruction. He rejected the teaching in architecture schools as without either practical or artistic usefulness, and he brazenly circularized those institutions for rebels who would welcome his "whole life" alternative. Applicants could expect the kind of inclusive experience that embraced both their spiritual and practical needs.

It was realized immediately that there were not enough accommodations for seventy apprentices — the plan had been to rebuild the Aunts' abandoned Hillside School, close by, but that would take time — so the number was reduced to thirty, with the fee raised to $1,100 within a year. All the places were filled immediately, with a waiting list, although Wright made it clear that applicants would be accepted or rejected at his pleasure; they, not the Fellowship, were on trial. He promised a utopian adventure, describing a democracy of fellows in which freedom and discipline got impossibly equal billing.

Once again, there are two versions from which to choose. The Fellowship was either a clever con game serving Wright's total self-interest, or a profound preparation for a life in architecture. It was a shameless scam, a form of indentured servitude that took advantage of those who hoped for, but never received, the promised architectural education, or a unique cultural and creative experience that brought the fortunate participant close to the eye and the hand and mind of one of the great artists of his time. It was an enlightened commune of like-minded companions developing healthy skills, or a rigid hierarchy ruled loosely by Wright and ruthlessly by Olgivanna, where no move or motive was unobserved or uncontrolled. Its detractors and defectors called it slavery, where the innocent victims labored — and paid — to give the lord of the manor an estate that he could not have otherwise afforded. There was no middle ground. Where some saw inspiration, others saw exploitation; some came and never left, while others departed as rapidly as possible.

Few great architects emerged; the work done at the Fellowship as the economy improved was all in Wright's shadow. Observers have suggested that the apprentice system failed to nurture and produce the same kind of talented practitioners who were drawn to Wright's studio earlier as paid employees: architects like Walter Burley Griffin and Marion Mahony and, later, Rudolf Schindler and Richard Neutra, who came, absorbed, contributed, and moved on. One of Wright's biographers, Robert Twombly, has charged that the Fellowship descended into a cult, and that the Wright scholarship that grew out of it became a controlled and redundant industry. The accusation is, in part, true; it was an inevitable devolution over time. But the Wright heritage owes an enormous debt to those believers and loyalists at the Fellowship and the Frank Lloyd Wright Foundation, which grew out of it, who became the caretakers of a historic heritage and priceless archive.

The Fellowship has been most sympathetically recorded by Edgar Tafel, an apprentice from 1932 to 1941, who became Wright's project manager on several important commissions, and left only when he was unable to resolve the matter of fee sharing for jobs that he brought in himself — a matter that Wright apparently never faced in a satisfactory manner. Tafel's recollections in his memoir *Years with Frank Lloyd Wright: Apprentice to Genius* are respectful, amusing, affectionate, and benign. Like the reverent references to "Mr. Jefferson" around Charlottesville, Virginia, no apprentice or associate, and no one at the Fellowship or Foundation, has ever referred to the master as anything but Mr. Wright. Tafel described how inexperienced apprentices fell off horses, broke limbs, cut and burned themselves using unfamiliar equipment, how Taliesin survived crisis after crisis. Nothing went smoothly, and Wright, undisturbed by continuous catastrophe, "didn't believe it should." He enjoyed "a stir" and, if none existed, would make one. Every shopping expedition was a confrontation in which he autocratically demanded, and got, bargains, or failing to do so, was blithely unembarrassed. He loved an audience, which the Fellowship unfailingly provided. Noting that he "was not the kind of man who can live alone and take care of himself," Tafel called Olgivanna the "stabilizing element" in Wright's life. It was she who ran the day-to-day operations and would "pick up all the pieces"; he never bothered himself with the trivia of how things worked.

Wright's image of Taliesin had not changed from his original concept twenty years earlier; he carried with him sentimental childhood memories of the valley's fruitful fields, contented herds, and brimming root cellars, of family picnics and summer tables groaning with a cornucopia of produce, honey, preserves, cakes, and pies. He expected these things to materialize magically and would call for picnics on short notice, certain that the apprentices would drop everything and appear with the same hampers of the fondly remembered foods, to be enjoyed in the familiar settings of his youth. Pictures show him in hat and linen trousers — lord of the picnic — presiding over young men and women seated on the ground in what appears to be more confusion than comfort. Trips would be taken on the spur of the moment in a variety of motorcars, apprentices commandeered as drivers, for absences of days, on sudden excursions.

Hospitality was bountiful at Taliesin. Visitors would be invited spontaneously, and weekends always brought guests in fluctuating numbers, often to Olgivanna's dismay. "Put more water in the soup!" Wright would cry cheerfully, as he prepared to enchant — or bore — a captive audience. Not surprisingly, fees failed to cover expenses. The apprentices instituted guided tours for a curious public, at ten cents a head, and after the Playhouse was built for amateur theatricals and Sunday movies — Wright adored movies — screenings were made available for the locals, who paid a nickel and were served doughnuts and coffee. None of this was much help for the permanently unbalanced books.

As a celebrity himself, Wright moved with the famous of his day. One regular guest at Taliesin was Alexander Woollcott, the *New Yorker* critic and Algonquin round table habitué, known for his caustic wit, who may have earned a particularly sumptuous summer breakfast by stating that if he had to reserve the word "genius" for one person, it would be for Wright. Strawberries with the dew still on them came in a pale green celadon bowl, followed by

farm-raised eggs and bacon, new aspar-
agus, fresh Guernsey milk, heavy cream,
and steaming coffee, served on an embroidered Chinese linen cloth, as ribbons of
morning mist dissolved in a brilliant,
sunny sky. The usually voluble Woollcott,
an ample man in polka-dot blue pa-
jamas — dots the size of saucers, Wright
noted — was silent as the sound of cow-
bells rose from the meadows below the
house and white peacocks called from the
terraces. All in this sylvan pastorale, recorded in enchanting detail by Wright in
the *Autobiography*, had, of course, been
raised, prepared, and tended by the apprentices.

Wright's snubs and insults to the European architects of the International style
are well known; one notorious incident has
him refusing to receive or speak to Walter
Gropius. In another rebuff, when it was
suggested that Le Corbusier would like to
visit Taliesin, Wright declined to see him.
He made exceptions — the Finnish architect Alvar Aalto and his wife were invited
"to spend a few days with us in the
country." Mies van der Rohe, newly arrived from Germany, was given an extensive tour of Wright's buildings that ended
at Taliesin; arriving for the day, he was

kept for three. His usually impeccable tailoring wilted, and his responses were reduced to *"Ja."*

But there would also be times when apprentices remembered eating little but cabbages and potatoes, or a particularly vile sauerkraut of Gurdjieff's devising — the guru visited in 1935 and left barrels of the stuff — but whatever the conditions, they carried on in style. On Sunday evenings, after extensive cleanup, all appeared for dinner in formal dress. Music followed and, almost always, spontaneous commentary by Wright. "Forty years later I remember his stories clearly because I loved the man so much," Tafel recalled. "And because I heard them so damned many times." Eventually, the fellowship of equals became a kind of royal court. In a curious denial of his vaunted egalitarian principles, Wright and Olgivanna presided over dinner and performances on a dais. Democracy, of which he often spoke and wrote, was a relative thing. At the same time that he celebrated the worth of the individual, he invented the term "mobocracy" for the anonymous, unenlightened masses unaware of his views. As he once explained wickedly to a Taliesin visitor, "We're very democratic here — when I'm hungry, everybody eats."

The Taliesin that Wright had come back to was in ruinous shape; an enormous amount of rebuilding was needed in addition to reclaiming the Hillside Home School for the Fellowship. Construction of the necessary facilities went slowly, and they were not completed until 1939. At the depths of the Depression, with massive unemployment, Wright, always without cash, was able to hire workmen for the promise of a small sum when the job was through. Not surprisingly, when President Franklin Roosevelt instituted the immediate payments of "relief," all left, and some sued for the amount they believed Wright owed them. He rationalized their claims as unfounded because the work was incomplete. In another monetary dispute, a man demanding settlement of an outstanding debt knocked him down and broke his nose. A group of loyal apprentices attempted a vigilante revenge, an escapade that ended in the local jail.

Without professional builders, the apprentices took over. Because no one would sell Wright lumber on credit, he contracted for green wood from local farmers in "cash only" deals, and the apprentices felled, hauled, and cut up the trees. When he could not afford the lime for mortar, they burned their own. Frustrated in his attempts to acquire stone from the local quarries — again, "cash only" was required and Wright didn't have it — they quarried it themselves, constructing walls under the direction of a local mason. Slowly the buildings grew, and so did "learning by doing" and the meaning of "tired on tired."

A column in the *Madison Capital Times* by the editor and writer Ernest L. Meyer, who spent some weeks with the Fellowship in 1934, describes activities at Taliesin with stunning immediacy. "The fragrance of fresh-hewn wood is in the wind, the smell of plaster, and the pungency of stone-dust under the chisel. Here is the uncompleted and vast drafting room . . . the public Playhouse, newly built . . . Phoenix in many forms winging out of the ashes of mischance. And the ashes are artfully mixed with the new. Buddhas and Chinese goddesses, snatched from the fire that once made Taliesin a husk, look from their perches in new stone walls. . . . The new Taliesin is bizarre and beautiful; in all the world there is nothing like it."

Driving tractors, tarring roofs, "picking sweet corn and digging onions in the hot sun," was followed by an afternoon break with pitchers of iced tea under the trees and "the sound of Brahms on a distant grand piano" — Wright had eleven grand pianos placed about the buildings. Next came the quieter pursuits of "paint, brush, and T-square." After dinner, a visit to the "newly-completed art gallery," where Meyer reports how Wright "lectures on Japanese prints" and "pleads with his apprentices to see . . . more than the surface of the world around them . . . to learn the peculiar genius or essence which makes a pine tree what it is . . . once they have probed the complex texture of the world, they can begin to interpret it through art and through building. . . . He speaks quietly, convincingly, directly, and with power."

Short-term observers like Meyer were enchanted by the offbeat curriculum and the chance to learn "the secrets of corn and cookery and cornice." Those who were not so enchanted saw favoritism, sycophancy, and a growing hierarchy of "ins" and "outs." There were feuds, affairs, and marriages, sometimes allegedly stage-managed by Olgivanna. One of the early apprentices, Wesley Peters, fell in love with Svetlana, Olgivanna's daughter by her first husband. When they married, they were banished briefly by the disapproving parents; on their return, Peters, an MIT-trained engineer, became Wright's invaluable assistant. Others, like Tafel and Eugene Masselink, who held Wright's life together as his secretary and personal assistant, and Bruce Brooks Pfeiffer, who remained to become the Taliesin archivist, arrived early and stayed with Wright for years. "We lived from hand to mouth at first and never had a fixed routine to cling to," Tafel recalled, "but we adored him nevertheless."

No one expected that Wright would reemerge as a powerful creative force, or that he was about to embark on an even more spectacular chapter of his life and career in a blaze of activity that he would sustain for another quarter of a century. Five years after the Fellowship was established, he would surprise the world with an amazing resurgence that would take him to a new level of achievement and fame.

10

Architects are not idle in fallow periods — they dream and draw. There is a whole body of work called visionary architecture produced at these times; it ranges from futuristic fantasies to cosmic city schemes. It demonstrates the best and the worst of the architectural mind-set — the soaring imagination of the artist, unrestricted by real limitations and conditions, producing designs of great beauty and originality, and the brilliant, often inhuman, socially naïve ideas of the utopian planner imposing a rigid physical order on the environment meant to sweep away the mess and ugliness of ordinary lives and places. It is easy to be carried away by the idealized logic of a theoretical urbanism presented in handsome drawings and impressive models, and architects tend to become attached to these ideas and images with a messianic intensity. But what often appears so attractively reasonable is totally unrelated to the political, social, and economic forces that are the true architects of cities.

Some of the most dramatic of these proposals, like Le Corbusier's 1925 Plan Voisin, would clearly have been disasters if it had been even remotely possible to carry them out. The Plan Voisin would have destroyed two square miles in the heart of Paris for eighteen freestanding skyscrapers bisected and served by superhighways, in a vast parklike setting with three levels of elevated pedestrian malls high among the trees. Seductive in the context of a decade infused with a belief in the perfectability of society through radical renewal, the plan would have replaced the intimate, event-filled humanity and historic and cultural diversity of one of the richest urban accretions in the world with a scaleless limbo of relentlessly imposed order and epic sterility.

Almost every architect plays this utopian game at some time. Wright had already expressed some of his planning ideas in *The Disappearing City*, published in 1932, in which he took a stand against traditional urban congestion in favor of a semirural, decentralized society in which every individual would have an acre of land to own and farm, and the unit of construction would be the single-family house. It was like Taliesin miniaturized and then writ large as the prototype, extended into a regional government of linked county units — city and town were simply eliminated. Churches, schools, administration buildings, and commercial structures were to be placed at strategic distances serving each region. He was not against a tall building in the right place — no architect is.

This bucolic dispersal of independent individuals would constitute a true democracy, in Wright's belief, an ideal made possible by the automobile that erased distances and opened new patterns of living and working. Wright championed the automobile from the very beginning; he loved it as a fast, flamboyant, and handsome toy in which he notoriously made his own rules of the road driving at consistently excessive speeds. Unlike Le Corbusier, however, who embraced a technological package of architecture, society, and contemporary life, Wright's utopian view was dominated by the use of the automobile as an instrument of flexibility and pleasure; its future as a generator of congestion and pollution and destroyer of cities was not yet apparent.

Wright called his scheme Broadacre City

and, as its name implied, this decentralized community looked back to the Jeffersonian agrarian ideal and away from later nineteenth-century industrial and urban concentration. As Neil Levine points out, with no work on the boards and a full complement of apprentices avid for the promised architectural experience to balance the utilitarian chores of house and barn, Broadacre City was a kind of private WPA project that Wright devised for the Fellowship during the Depression. Not surprisingly, it was the polar opposite of the Corbusian ideal — a far gentler urbanism, if it could be called urbanism at all. It was conceived in terms of familiar American practices of building and land use. A large twelve-foot-square model was constructed and exhibited in 1935 at New York's Rockefeller Center, about as far from Wright's decentralized dream of an individualized, democratic patrimony as possible, in a city that he often claimed to despise — an irony that seems to have escaped viewers and commentators. The model traveled to Washington and Pittsburgh and was an instant source of the kind of attention that kept Wright in the public eye.

In addition to its value as publicity and

its use as an educational project to induct the apprentices into Wright's way of working and thinking, Broadacre City was the generator of the Usonian house — Wright's single-family home that was quickly and successfully adapted by builders as the ranch house, the most rational, reasonable, and popular American home of the twentieth century. The name Usonian has been explained variously by Wright and others; it is wordplay on usefulness and the USA and was meant to imply an organic, natural house that would respect the land and indigenous materials. The design was replicable, affordable, and adaptable to almost any site or situation. Wright always stressed the house's democratic and universal nature and claimed that it could be built for $5,000 to $10,000.

The brilliance of the Usonian house is the way in which it recognized the changes taking place in American society and domestic life. Its immediate appeal helped bring Wright back into active practice. Practical, reasonable, and far above the common level of builder design, the Usonian house attracted enlightened clients of the type that Wright usually dealt with — well-educated professionals and intellectuals in middle-class communities. It was directed at an emerging lifestyle of a generation living a simpler, more mobile, and much less formal life, reflecting the changing role of women in America, who were pursuing more varied activities, entertaining without servants, and controlling the household in a new way that required greater functional ease and freedom.

This was a distinct departure from the Prairie house, Wright's revolutionary design of the turn of the century that reduced the complexities of Victorian living to radically reconceived open and flowing spaces. The Usonian house was often L-shaped. It retained the traditional hearth and fireplace, but it dispensed with the formal dining room and the servants' wing. A dining area in the living room connected directly with the kitchen, where the two wings met. The bedroom wing, when set at an angle to the living quarters, framed an outdoor area serving both. A carport, which Wright also claimed to have invented, completed the Usonian design.

The prototype of the Usonian house was built in Minneapolis for a professor of sociology, Malcolm Willey, and his wife, in 1933–1934. It led to many similar houses — single-story, brick and wood structures with warm wood interiors and brick or stone fireplaces, ranges of windows and walls of glass doors leading to patios or terraces outside. Among the most celebrated and publicized of these houses were those built for the Jacobs, Lewis, Baird, Pope, and Hanna families. Some, like the Jacobses and Lewises, who felt that their houses changed their lives in extraordinary ways, wrote books about the experience. A few even commissioned a second house as their families grew. Not everyone loved them, however, or was converted to Wright's overriding aesthetic or ideas about living. Over the years, there have been owners who have felt imprisoned by their houses, acting as Wright's reluctant "caretakers." Annoyed by a steady stream of architectural voyeurs, they have fled for more accommodating and anonymous quarters. Much has been written about the difficulties and disruption and rising costs of Wright's unconventional construction and the frustrations of a cantankerous and often absent or unavailable architect, who would appear just often enough to charm and appease the desperate client.

But Wright's houses never insisted that their occupants reshape themselves to conform to an abstract architectural ideal. Although he was relentlessly dictatorial about building in furniture of his own design and including his own accessories — he was known to go into his houses during the owners' absence and rearrange everything to his taste — and some of that furniture was notoriously uncomfortable, he never adopted the functional minimalism promoted for low-cost dwellings by the International style. His houses are positively *gemütlich* compared with the enforced antisepsis that has reached a challenging astringency as the architectural avant-garde strives for a reductive perfection. Usonian houses were, and are, inviting and livable. Those who commissioned them knew what they were getting and, even when they received the unexpected, like Wright's later hexagonal plans, which included matching tables that tipped and stools that fell, as he increasingly played with geometry, they rolled with the punches, or angles.

By the mid-1930s, the type was well established, and Wright was ready for a far greater domestic challenge. This came with the commission for Fallingwater, the house over a waterfall in the woods at Bear Run, Pennsylvania, which became one of the most famous and admired houses in the world. The client, who appeared fortuitously at this time, was Edgar J. Kaufmann, the wealthy owner of a Pittsburgh department store whose interest in art and style, and particularly in architecture, led him to Wright in late 1934.

Like so much else in Wright's life, there are two starkly different versions of how Kaufmann got there. The standard account is the one told by Kaufmann's son, Edgar Kaufmann Jr. In his early twenties, young Edgar had been studying art and design in Vienna. On his return to the United States, as he tells it, he was given a copy of Wright's *Autobiography* by a friend, which led to his recommendation of Wright to his father, as well as a subsequent stay at the Taliesin Fellowship. According to his story, the three men — father, son, and Wright — visited the site together, and the decision to hire Wright was made through the son's suggestion and intervention. A revisionist account is given by Franklin Toker, an architectural historian who has delved deeply into the people and circumstances involved. In *Fallingwater Rising*, Toker claims that Edgar Jr. maximized his role, or at least fudged his account. He offers evidence that the younger

Kaufmann was not present at that initial site visit, and his research finds no trace of anyone resembling the person who supposedly supplied the Wright *Autobiography*. Toker claims that these discrepancies invalidate Edgar Jr.'s account and commonly accepted role. According to Toker, the shoe was on the other foot — the elder Kaufmann's, in fact; he calls the father the motivating force whose own interests led him to Wright without his son's assistance. He also believes that it was the elder Kaufmann who directed his son to Wright, rather than the other way around, insisting that he join the Taliesin Fellowship, which he claims the young man disliked, staying only briefly and failing miserably to get along with anyone, including Wright, who was so secure in his relationship with the elder Kaufmann that he felt free to treat young Edgar with contempt.

The background for both versions, and the reality, are undoubtedly more complex. The tension and antagonism between father and son cannot be overstated. Edgar Kaufmann Sr. was an extremely successful and powerful man of strong opinions, tastes, and actions, who treated his son as a disappointment; he approved of neither his style nor his homosexual orientation.

He was flagrantly unfaithful to young Edgar's mother, his wife, Liliane, to the delight of the popular press and the boy's shamed distress, and he married one of his mistresses after his wife's death. His richly flamboyant life, his conspicuous sensuality, were always anathema to his son, who maintained a highly cultivated, intensely reserved, and carefully understated aestheticism. He was as private and ascetic as his father was worldly and self-indulgent. He refused to capitalize the "junior" in his name, spelling it jr., and did his best to drop it at his father's death.

Edgar Kaufmann Jr. was a man of great intelligence and extremely fine-tuned sensibilities, refined, sophisticated and somewhat perverse in his tastes, with strong passions and a violent temper. He practiced a conspicuous self-restraint and an impeccable politesse that came initially from good breeding, but was cultivated in all of his professional and personal relationships. Later in life, as the possessor of great wealth, he could be generous and kind. He was well known and highly respected as a teacher and tastemaker in art and design in the museum, academic, and commercial worlds; his philanthropy focused on the exhibitions, publications, and educational undertakings with which he was involved. One could logically assume that he was neither the dispensable wimp that Toker portrays nor the unblemished hero of his own story. As with almost everything in Wright's debatable history, we are free to choose what we like, or what matters.

In the end, the brilliance of the building beggars both accounts. The famous view of Fallingwater that has been endlessly reproduced is a breathtaking image — a cascade of concrete balconies hanging magically over a stream above a waterfall. It is a rare instance of art not diminishing nature, but enriching it; the house completes the natural, rocky, wooded slope and creates a perfect counterpoint to it. What appears in the photograph as a flat, abstract composition of sliding planes is a complex, three-dimensional structure of interlocking and intricately balanced volumes, like trays on a waiter's fingers, as Wright liked to say, held together and anchored by a vertical stone tower. The cantilevered trays, separated by continuous glass windows in metal sash, contain the rooms and their open balcony extensions. There is another set of falls, just downstream beyond the picture; the camera's dramatic but static view only hints at the subtle, changing connections of the house, the rushing water, and the seasonally transformed site.

Wright ignored the normal solution that would have placed the house away from the stream with a view of the falls; building it over the stream, instead, was a daring design decision that challenged customary ideas and conventional construction. He fastened it to the rock with concrete "bolsters," but the symbolic anchor is inside — a huge boulder that has been carefully retained by the hearth in a large living area about thirty-eight by forty-eight feet. The ceiling, as was Wright's custom, is held low in relation to the size of the room. Even at this size, however, the room has a rustic intimacy. A floor of waxed local stone leads to the terraces and to an open hatch with a flight of steps down to the stream below. The house is both above and of the stream, and connected directly to it.

Although there are precedents for Fallingwater in his own work, a new vision is present in those hovering, abstract, concrete slabs. There is a clear connection to the European modernism that Wright spurned; he had obviously studied it, although the application he chose to make was organic in its relationship to the natural site. Unlike European buildings that maintained a cool aloofness from their surroundings, Wright's slabs were tied to the earth, physically and symbolically, with rough local stone and natural textures and colors. The Museum of Modern Art's exhibition devoted to Fallingwater in 1938 used photographs in which the slabs looked almost white; the way the museum presented the building, not surprisingly, emphasized its International style bias. But Wright never saw those floating planes as white. He had originally wanted gold leaf applied to the balconies, but when that was considered too richly ostentatious, he settled on a warm, apricot-toned beige paint. Instead of the stark industrial metal trim of the International style, he used his favorite Cherokee red. His grasp of a new architectural era was complete, even as he denounced its practitioners. But his design was driven directly and deeply by the presence and spirit of the superb setting; in Neil Levine's perfect summary, Fallingwater "is ultimately about the cumulative effect of stone, water, trees, leaves, mist, clouds, and sky."

Legend has it that the house was designed almost instantaneously, under the pressure of an impending visit from Kaufmann, who had been waiting impatiently for drawings. Although Wright had made two site visits to Pennsylvania months earlier and had requested and received topographical maps, he had apparently drawn nothing. When a call came from Kaufmann announcing that he was in Milwaukee and would be arriving at Taliesin shortly to see the design, Wright announced that the house was finished. "Come along, E.J.," he boomed, "we're ready for you!" According to Edgar Tafel and other apprentices who witnessed the incident, Wright sat down at the drafting table and the house poured out of him as he talked aloud, explaining exactly how it would be situated, what it would look like and how it would be used, where the owners would sit and the things they would see, even the way the water would be boiled for tea in a red kettle suspended from the hearth. Plans, elevations, and sections appeared in rapid succession, and he finished, triumphantly, just as Kaufmann arrived.

Wright liked to say he shook his designs out of his sleeve, like a magician, but he had obviously been thinking about this one for months. All architects have the power of visualization; few would sit down to a blank piece of paper with a blank mind. Wright possessed the ability to conceptualize and visualize a total solution to a problem to an exceptional degree. It was not unusual for him to have a fully conceived plan long before committing it to paper. Nor is it surprising that those who have doubted the story and looked in vain for preliminary sketches have not found them. Wright's concept of Fallingwater must have been clear before he drew a line. Beyond this initial client presentation, however, there would be many more detailed drawings and specifications; problems arising from the radical nature of the building would have to be resolved during construction, a practice that could prove frustrating and costly for both client and builder.

The remarkable design of Fallingwater was recognized instantly as a work of art; it also produced a host of immediate problems. Cracks and structural faults appeared before the house was complete, and Kaufmann commissioned his own engineering studies, which enraged Wright, who threatened to quit. A game ensued of secret reinforcements, orders given and rescinded by both client and architect, accompanied by a lively, idiosyncratic correspondence. But it was a confluence of predictable and unpredictable circumstances that led eventually to the building's near collapse almost sixty years later. The largely empirical and untested nature of the engineering calculations used for the unconventional structure, essential steel that was left out of the window framing under the bedroom cantilever, concrete that was inadequately or improperly reinforced, and shaky supervision during construction by inexperienced apprentices forced to make critical decisions on the spot, often caused by Wright's failure to supply drawings as needed, were all contributing factors. Many of these faults and omissions were not discovered until later repairs revealed them. All were accidents or oversights that increased the risks of a design so far beyond standard practice that only materials and techniques available today would have guaranteed its successful execution.

After his parents' death, Edgar Kaufmann Jr. used the house and maintained it superbly for many years. He donated the house and the land to the Western Pennsylvania Conservancy in 1963, more than two decades before his own death, in order to establish and ensure proper standards of preservation and presentation when it would be opened to the public. A national landmark, it has become a major tourist attraction. A total retrofitting of the house was undertaken in the 1990s, not only to correct the much publicized, dangerously sagging cantilevers, but also to replace the old and outmoded plumbing, heating, and electrical systems originally meant only for family use, but by then suffering from age and the unanticipated stresses of tourism.

In 2000, the American Institute of Architects voted Fallingwater the Building of the Century. The accolade came forty-one years after Wright's death, following a lifetime of open warfare with the institute, during which he constantly insulted and alienated his peers. When they finally gave him the institute's Gold Medal, he was eighty-two (admitting to eighty) and he berated them roundly at the presentation ceremony.

As luck and fate would have it, two ideal clients came to Wright in the 1930s, bringing the major projects that would reinvigorate his practice. The first was Edgar Kaufmann, whose Fallingwater gave Wright the means and opportunity to design an extraordinary house; the second

282

was Herbert F. Johnson, the head of the Johnson Wax Company, who commissioned the one thing Wright's practice lacked at that time: a large commercial building — an administration headquarters for the family-owned business in Racine, Wisconsin. Both men became more than clients; they were patrons who supported Wright in many ways. Kaufmann gave funds toward the production of the Broadacre City model and had Wright design his stylishly modern office at the store, later acquired by the Victoria and Albert Museum. Hib Johnson became his champion and close personal friend.

Wright began work on the Johnson Administration Building in 1936 while he was still deeply involved with the development of Fallingwater. He tried to persuade Johnson to move the building into the country, Broadacre City style, and when Johnson refused, Wright shut out the surrounding industrial neighborhood, much as he had done with the Larkin Building in Buffalo many years earlier. As in the Larkin Building, the interior is a vast, open, balconied room that served as the main work space, with administration offices in the balconies above. Also following the Larkin model, the furnishings and fittings were all Wright-designed. But unlike the severe and solidly monumental Larkin, the Johnson Building was light and elegant, "streamlined" in the latest taste, in aggressive denial of Wright's advancing age. Where the curved corners met the ceiling, a flowing line of glass tubing — a new, experimental material that had never been employed in this fashion before — admitted a wash of light. Tapering columns made an enchanted architectural forest; more columns were used than were structurally necessary, to increase the effect. Light rising from their lily-pad tops dematerialized the room. It is a timeless, magical space.

The glass tubing was untested and, inevitably, it leaked. Wright's enthusiasm for new materials and unproven methods of construction had creative advantages for him that far outweighed any discomfort for his clients. Faced with his airy unconcern, they learned to deal with experimental systems like the radiant heating in his houses that soon became standard building practice. The columns, which tapered from top to bottom with an amazing delicacy, were mistrusted by the local building authorities, and with his usual bravado, Wright held a public test for officials and company executives. Sandbags were piled high on a sample column, far in excess of the required weight-bearing capacity, until it crashed — dramatic proof of Wright's self-professed infallibility. The construction of the Administration Building never received more than a conditional building permit, but it went ahead, in part because Hib Johnson personally backed his architect at all board and commission hearings.

With the Administration Building well along, Wright designed Wingspread, a house for Johnson and his recent bride. Built in Racine in 1937, it was as specific to its prairie site as Fallingwater was to its stream and woodland setting. Four zones, or "wings," extended from a high "wigwam"-like central room, where a soaring brick chimney provided fireplaces for each projecting wing. But the house was destined never to be fully lived in; when it was almost complete, Johnson's young wife died, and he lost interest in its construction. It was only at Wright's urging that it was finished. He was loath to lose a design of such importance to him, and he noted that, with the building done, the site seemed "to come alive." Wright liked to believe that the house helped Johnson heal, although his residence was short and clearly unhappy. Eventually, the building was used as a conference center.

As Wright's celebrity escalated, public activities took more of his time. He was invited to attend the All-Union Congress of Soviet Architects in the Soviet Union in 1937, returning with a naïvely enthusiastic view of the future of communism and Soviet architecture, an opinion shared by other artists and intellectuals who visited in that decade. The 1938 exhibition of Fallingwater at the Museum of Modern Art in New York gave Wright instant, unassailable cachet. He edited a special issue of a leading professional publication, *Architectural Forum*, featuring his work, and in a testament to his growing fame and media compatibility, he appeared on the cover of *Time* magazine. That same year, another client who became a committed patron, Dr. Ludd M. Spivey, brought him a long-term institutional commission — the design of Florida Southern College in Lakeland, Florida. Wright gave a series of lectures in London in 1939, which he published as *An Organic Architecture* and helped prepare an exhibition of his work that the Museum of Modern Art mounted in 1940, shown with D. W. Griffith, under the title "Two Great Americans."

It was a heavy schedule for a man in his seventies, and after a serious bout with pneumonia, he was told to avoid the harsh Wisconsin winters, a suggestion that sent him back to the Arizona desert that he loved. Not only could he escape the cold by a seasonal transfer of his activities, but he would also save $3,500 in winter fuel costs, a substantial and always problematic sum. After looking at a number of possibilities, he acquired about 600 acres on the Maricopa Mesa in the Paradise Valley, not far from Phoenix and Scottsdale, small resort communities at that time. Part of the site was bought from the Government Land Office; the rest was leased. As the Fellowship doubled from thirty to more than sixty apprentices, he bought additional land, eventually owning more than 1,000 acres. He described the site, a high desert plateau against a backdrop of the MacDowell Range, as "a look over the rim of the world," and ignored the fact that no water had ever been found there. With his usual assurance that he could not be wrong and that his luck would not fail him, he ordered continuous drilling until water miraculously appeared.

The yearly trip to Arizona made by family and apprentices, known as the "migration," "trek," or "hegira," began in 1937. A motorcade of cars and trucks, with Wright and his family in the lead in his current favorite, would leave Taliesin around Christmas and return to Wisconsin after Easter. Wright enjoyed the approximately 2,000-mile trip, dictating varying and circuitous routes. Construction of the Desert Camp, as it was called at the start — for which Ocatilla had been the dress rehearsal — began in early 1938, and after four winters of seasonal building by the apprentices and some hired labor it was essentially complete in 1941, although additions and revisions never stopped. After flirtations with all sorts of nomenclature, it was simply called Taliesin West.

They camped out during construction in sleeping bags and temporary tents, enduring heat, cold, sandstorms, and seasonal floods under the most primitive conditions. Plans were drawn in the open air under the endless sky, with brown butcher paper substituted for white drafting stock to temper the blinding brilliance of the sun and the strong desert light. "Certain forms already abounded," Wright noted in the revised edition of the *Autobiography*, "simple characteristic silhouettes . . . drifts and heaps of sunburned rocks. . . . We devised a light canvas-covered redwood framework resting on this massive stone masonry belonging to the mountain slopes all around."

They soon found that the land had been used ceremonially for centuries by Native American tribes. The low, one-story complex was oriented to the historical and mythical features of the landscape as well as to its visible physical aspects. Wright adopted the squared spiral of the petroglyphs left on huge boulders by the Hohokam and used it for the Fellowship logo. The boulders themselves were transported to serve as markers and sculpture in the camp after careful compass readings were taken to reproduce their orientation. If the Hohokam were to return, Wright said, they would find things undisturbed. The drafting room, dining hall, residences, living and garden rooms, Wright's office and family quarters, were unified but independent structures joined by a connecting platform, terraces, bridges, steps, pools, patios, and carefully orchestrated mountain views. The hexagonal plan created a dynamic flow of triangular spaces that culminated in an angled prow thrusting into the desert.

As the camp rose from the desert, it disappeared into it; the walls, piers, and parapets were made of what Wright called "desert rubble stone," fragments of varying color and size collected from the site and bound together in molds with a light cement. Rough-sawn redwood, stained brown, formed fins to support the canvas roofs, slanted to reflect the angle of the mountains. "On a fair day," Wright recorded, "when those white tops and side flaps were flung open the desert air and the birds flew clear through. There was a belfry and a big bell. There were gardens. One a great prow running out onto the Mesa overlooking the world, wide desert below, a triangular pool nesting in it. . . . Our new desert camp belonged to the Arizona desert as though it had stood here during creation." With the passage of time, the suburbs of Phoenix and Scottsdale moved so close that Wright's careful preparatory processional through the desert was lost. And as time and climate took their toll, steel and plastic replaced wood and canvas, but the dramatic, allegorical nature of the siting and design still held.

As with many of Wright's buildings, any investigation of its rationale or sources brings one back to the fact that it is indeed unique — an extraordinary achievement of the most personal kind. But it is not novelty that accounts for its special genius and universal fame; it is the poetic expression of a site-specific solution inspired by the desert itself. The design's unusual character was based on more than the architect as rebellious, romantic loner; as usual, Wright was closely attuned to contemporary developments. A surge of interest in archaeology and Indian affairs in the 1930s was followed by government reforms and scholarly digs that interpreted and elevated Native American culture as a major part of the Mesoamerican tradition. Neil Levine has pointed out that Wright's already existing interest in prehistoric cultures allied naturally with modernism's growing emphasis on the "primitive" as a fresh source of vision. Wright extolled the "true values" of those who lived simply, with nature. There was no culture too distant or art too esoteric, nothing too sophisticated or elementary, too new or too old, to be subsumed into his idea of an appropriate and indigenous way of building. In the desert, he had even created his own world.

11

"Truth against the world" and "Wright against the world" were now one thing. In the Taliesins of Wisconsin and Arizona, his separation from society, his rejection of its standards and insulation from its demands, was complete. But if he was a prophet in the Arizona desert and continued to preach from it, he was no recluse; he loved the world stage and managed to stay on it. He relished the limelight; having created his persona, he dressed for the part in tweeds and capes and flowing ties and his trademark porkpie hat, made for him by Charvet in Paris, gray hair at a properly picturesque length. His gestures were large and dramatic; he wielded his cane with insolent panache. His voice was unmistakable — the fine, deep voice of an actor, with timbre and resonance, and he delighted in using it to shock, surprise, and amuse. He could charm and insult with equal expertise and enjoyed doing both. He understood the part he was playing perfectly and exploited it with consummate skill.

He had plenty of onstage opportunities as the drumroll of honors accelerated in the late 1930s and continued for the next twenty years. The praise and publicity that accompanied his most recent work served as a reminder of his earlier achievements. He accepted the recognition as an entitlement, although he felt it should have come sooner, and lost no opportunity to scold his admirers, reassert his genius, and accuse others of appropriating his ideas. He was awarded the Gold Medal of the Royal Institute of British Architects in 1941 but did not receive a similar honor in his own country until eight years later. He was made an honorary member of the National Academy of Architects in Uruguay and Mexico, the National Academy of Finland, the Royal Academy of Fine Arts in Stockholm, and the National Academy and Institute of Arts and Letters at home. He collected honorary degrees from Princeton, Yale, Wesleyan, Florida Southern College, the University of Wisconsin (at long last!), and the Eidgenossische Technische Hochschule of Zurich.

At Taliesin, he was the master of a realm of his own making, surrounded by those who had come to learn his ways. What was happening outside of this world was irrelevant; the rise of Hitler and the imminence of war seemed part of another cosmos. Both on the Midwestern farm with its unfailing seasonal rhythms and in the clear air of the remote desert camp, the growing storm could be easily ignored or relegated to the back of Wright's accommodating mind. The total immersion of the artist in the work at hand, an unquestioning belief in its primacy in the universal scheme of things, is the common currency of genius. His prejudices and opinions became absolute and automatic, undiluted by doubts, undisturbed by any new or revised information.

Wright presented the classic dilemma of the great artist — large in his art, but small in his attitudes — a phenomenon that has always puzzled those who persist in believing that the human dimension should match the artist's creative gifts. They rarely do; character and creativity run on separate tracks. Wright was as vulnerable to bad action and bad judgment as any ordinary mortal. He convinced himself that there would be no war; he rationalized his objections in part because he feared its impact on the Fellowship. If the young men left who had made his home, farm, and studio a going concern, he would lose what he had so carefully constructed.

But there was much in his background and beliefs that contributed to his antiwar stand. Two generations removed from the flight of his Welsh antecedents from the poverty and oppressive laws of English rule and the family's persecution as a dissenting Unitarian sect by the Church of England, he still shared the family bias — he was openly anti-English, which translated into opposing the American-British alliance in both world wars. A product of the American heartland, he was unreservedly conservative in spite of his flamboyant displays of unconventional personal morality and parlor radicalism. A staunch isolationist, he joined America First, although it is unlikely that he shared that notorious group's more unsavory agenda; he was too politically inattentive.

His taste and attachments had been formed as a young man in Chicago's dominant Germanic culture at the end of the nineteenth century. He rejected the powerful and fashionable influence of the Ecole des Beaux-Arts and Paris never interested him as much as Berlin and Vienna. In addition to his anti-British and pro-German stand in the Second World War, he was pro-Japanese. But what he loved, he explained in the *Autobiography*, was the *old* Germany, and the *old* Japan; to him, these were not the countries that were now the enemy. His association with Japan and its people, and his love of its art and culture, went back thirty years, and much of his livelihood depended on his role as a collector and dealer in Japanese prints.

There has been speculation that he was anti-Semitic, based on comments and quotations from his writings. While he had categorized some of his early drafting room companions in the Adler and Sullivan office unflatteringly as Jews, he did not spare those of other religious or ethnic identity — he expressed equal distaste for them all. His respect and liking for Dankmar Adler, the brilliant German Jewish engineering partner of Adler and Sullivan, was unreserved. So was his attachment to young Jewish architects like Edgar Tafel, an apprentice and friend, even after he left the Fellowship. It is difficult to believe that anti-Semitism figured seriously in Wright's ritual obsessions. Some of his best and most loyal clients and patrons for whom he did his finest work were Jews, like the Kaufmanns and the Guggenheims, who paralleled his earlier affluent, liberal Wasp clients, but had money and ambition on a larger scale. His personal relationships were warm with the upper-middle-class Jewish teachers and intellectuals who built his Usonian houses. Wright's long list of fools and rogues made no distinctions of race or ethnicity; he was uniformly politically incorrect.

He was unaware of any paradox in his beliefs or attitudes. At the same time that he was fiercely loyal to his ideal vision of America, his politics — if the word can be used for something as ad hoc and ill formed as Wright's views — followed confused and irrational lines. He was used to saying what he thought, regardless of facts or logic. Not surprisingly, the young and impressionable apprentices, absorbed by the excitement and immediacy of their architectural mission and the closed, paternalistic atmosphere of the Fellowship, were not immune to the Master's often expressed ideas, which embraced the broadly and fuzzily philosophical as much as they addressed building beliefs and practices. In Wright's mind, the two were indivisible and, with his inherited talents as a preacher, his antiwar sentiments had some effect on his listeners, and even reached government ears. He claimed that he influenced no one, and had no intention of doing so; he said that those who came to him did so because they already had similar views.

In this introverted society, focused solely on its artistic pursuits, the advent of World War II was greeted with dismay. Called up by the draft to serve in a war that seemed so distant and irrelevant against the timelessness of art and desert, a number of the apprentices declared themselves conscientious objectors and served time in jail. Wright once more found himself embroiled with the law, this time the Sedition Act of 1918, passed during the First World War to punish those "who interfered with the war effort," or "spoke disloyally of the United States Constitution or Federal government." A local judge dealing with the Fellowship's conscientious objectors viewed Wright's commune as a hotbed of traitorous anti-Americanism. Diplomacy was not Wright's long suit. His denials included righteous statements of his convictions bound to irritate and make things worse.

One young objector's parents, deeply upset by their son's defiance of the draft, carried accusations against Wright to the FBI, where they received the personal attention of J. Edgar Hoover, who quickly deemed Wright a threat to national security, or at least believed that he was fomenting a revolution at Taliesin. Wright's naïvely enthusiastic endorsement of Soviet communism, with the exception of its official architecture — he deplored the kitsch classicism of the Palace of the Soviets and tried with characteristic hubris to influence its design during his 1937 visit — could not have helped his case. Hoover recommended that action be taken against Wright for sedition, but a federal assistant attorney general refused to prosecute — not once, but twice.

Comic relief was provided by Ayn Rand, a writer who had emigrated from the Soviet Union and had plans to write a novel about an architect, inspired by articles she had read by and about Wright. The book she subsequently published, *The Fountainhead*, was a wildly successful best seller and then a movie starring Gary Cooper; the architect-hero, Howard Roark, commonly believed to be modeled on Frank Lloyd Wright, has made generations of young women swoon. Roark is portrayed as a brilliantly creative, fiery genius, embattled by the establishment, who defiantly blows up his consummate work of art, a skyscraper, rather than see his talent and integrity compromised. Wright never felt any real affinity with the fictional Roark and at first rejected any identification with the character — except for the talent and integrity part. He said that Rand failed to understand him and that she never got it right. When asked if he was the model for Roark, he replied, "I deny the paternity and refuse to marry the mother." Only after the book and its hero became sensationally popular did he allow that perhaps he could identify with the impossibly arrogant and idealistic Roark. As Meryle Secrest perceived, Rand was pretty far off the mark — Wright would never have blown up one of his own buildings.

Rand left the Soviet Union so disillusioned by communism that she espoused a theory of individualism, called objectivism, that celebrated the virtues of unbridled self-interest and the glories of a rampantly free capitalism. She was not at all in tune with Wright's blissfully innocent belief that Soviet communism was a kind of benevolent democracy for the masses. There was a yawning gap between many of their ideas. Her first efforts to see him were frustrated; when she wrote, in 1937, professing her admiration and asking for an appointment, she received a letter addressed to "Mr."

Rand, saying that Wright had no time. She finally succeeded in arranging a meeting when Wright gave a talk in New York in late 1938; as reported in detail in the Secrest biography, Rand went to Bonwit Teller on Fifth Avenue and spent a lavish and, for her, unprecedented $350 for a glamorous black velvet dress, shoes, and cape for the occasion. There is no evidence that Wright was impressed. He tolerated her attention over the next decade, but she was as opinionated as he was, and her visits to Taliesin were a trial. He designed a house for her in the 1940s that she never built, preferring to buy, at considerably less cost, an existing house the Austrian American Richard Neutra had built for Josef von Sternberg; by now, Wright considered his former employee an archenemy. On her final visit to Taliesin, she smoked so heavily that he threw her cigarette in the fire and ordered her to leave. He imposed a ban on smoking at Taliesin from then on.

A more welcome distraction was the arrival of Solomon R. Guggenheim, the wealthy art collector who planned to build a new museum in New York — the structure that was to become Wright's most contentious creation and the masterwork of his late years. The design of the Solomon R. Guggenheim Museum was developed from 1943 to 1945. Solomon Guggenheim died in 1949, and it is doubtful that the museum would ever have been built if its construction had not been stipulated in his will. Work did not start until 1956, and the building was completed only in 1959, six months after Wright died.

What we see today, and this was the case from the time the doors opened, is not the museum Wright and his client had in mind. Solomon Guggenheim's museum was purpose-designed to fit a radical idea of how art should be displayed, based on an extreme form of abstract painting in the 1940s called "non-objective" art. After Guggenheim's death, the highly idiosyncratic museum that Wright created in painstaking collaboration with his patron's ideas was turned into another kind of museum, fighting back all the way. It kept its basic form, but the original concept that the form served was abandoned. The transformation that took place in how the building is used is the cause of many of its well-publicized problems. The museum has been under attack by critics and curators ever since, unaware of the sources of the trouble and unwilling to acknowledge them. But the iconic form of the

Guggenheim is so powerful, and essentially indestructible, that it has survived the corruption of its purpose to become an international landmark — long before Frank Gehry's Bilbao Guggenheim achieved that status.

The practitioners of non-objective art believed that they had freed painting from all references to recognizable objects, for an artistic breakthrough that superseded the reflections of the real world that artists have traditionally produced. They claimed to have created a new kind of reality that extended pictorial space beyond the picture frame into real space, and that any division between the two ceased to exist. By experiencing paintings in this new way, the theory went — in a sense, by becoming part of them — viewers could reach a new understanding of art and reality. The harmony thus achieved would become a feeling of inner serenity, of oneness with the world, which, if universally practiced, could lead to world peace. Or so Solomon Guggenheim was willing to believe, under the tutelage of a young German artist, the Baroness Hilla Rebay, whose persuasive skills had converted him to the cause of the non-objective art that he now collected exclusively.

Wright was asked to design a building that would serve this new and different way of seeing and understanding art. Rebay described it as a "temple" where a transcendental revelation would take place. As director and curator, she was to have a penthouse apartment in its upper reaches for as long as she lived. When both she and Solomon Guggenheim died, the collection would be frozen, nothing ever added, subtracted, or changed. This wildly over-reaching concept of art as a mystical route to everything from spiritual self-realization to peace among nations was promoted by Rebay with messianic conviction and Guggenheim's backing and money.

He had already amassed an impressive collection of canvases by the best non-objective artists, Wassily Kandinsky, Max Ernst, Jean Arp, and Hans Richter, work that has stood the test of time and the disappearance of its bizarre theories, as well as a disproportionate number by a lesser member of the group, Rudolf Bauer, whom Rebay particularly favored. In the collection's temporary, pre-Wright quarters in a midtown Manhattan town house, the pictures floated in a luminous glow against pleated gray fabric, close to the gray-carpeted floor, the hushed galleries broken only by softly piped-in classical mood music. The design and installation were meant to lull the visitor into a state of passive receptivity to the paintings' spiritual presence and message.

When Rebay contacted Wright, she clearly expected him to go beyond the conventional norms of museum design. With his Emersonian background and beliefs, he was no stranger to the transcendental. He was not, however, about to create some cloud-cuckoo-land. What he took as his mandate was second nature to him — a release from convention, the freedom to redefine a building type, in this case to rethink the art museum in an unprecedented way. He was well practiced in this kind of reconfiguration and, not surprisingly, he found some of the rethinking he had already been doing was instantly applicable, either by good fortune or, more likely, because he willed it to be so. He returned to an idea that had preoccupied him for many years: the search for a plastic, sculptural architecture that would be unbroken by conventional walls and floors, where mass and space were one — a concept that was to become architecture's leading edge by the end of the twentieth century.

The continuous spiral surrounding a great unitary space was a repeated theme in Wright's work from the time of the unbuilt plans for the Automobile Objective and Planetarium of 1924–1925; it appeared again much later in the Morris Shop in San Francisco, built in 1948–1949. This does not imply a lack of ideas or laziness, as some critics like to assume; there are ideas with a creative potential and multiple applications that fascinate architects, themes that they explore and develop throughout a career. The great central space surrounded by balconies can be seen even earlier in the Larkin Building of 1902–1906 and Unity Temple in 1905–1908, and still later in the Johnson Administration Building of 1936. The search for a plastic, free-flowing architecture with spaces that interact on many levels preoccupied him throughout his career, but architecture's more sculptural aspects would not be fully explored until computer-assisted drawing made it possible to plot complex shapes with astounding structural and economic accuracy. As usual, Wright was pushing design and technology far into the future. The spiral, the circle, the dome, and the cantilever dominated much of his late work, in churches, community facilities, and public buildings. He added *Arabian Nights* imagery to a proposed cultural center for Baghdad, and Native American motifs for a state capitol design that he offered in vain to donate to his adopted Arizona; perhaps state officials could not visualize themselves in tipis.

The only material available in the 1940s that could produce the sculptural shapes Wright sought was the still relatively new one of reinforced concrete, formed painstakingly in wooden molds. The structural calculations for curved surfaces departed radically from those used for "the stratified layers of post and beam," as Wright put it; the change from straight-lined and rectilinear, he explained, had to be figured in terms of "the cantilever and continuity." But without the computer, and with far less advanced materials and techniques, the technology of the 1940s and '50s was often inadequate to the task. With all of its imperfections, however, the Guggenheim stands as an acknowledged model and inspiration for those architects who later did the most creative work.

From the outside, the Guggenheim Museum looks like a cyclinder, or an inverted ziggurat once one notices the outward slant to the top. A series of stacked volumes grow wider as they rise to a glass dome; these layers are separated by a continuous glass band meant to bring daylight to the spiral ramp inside. A ledge along the ramp was to be used like an easel for the display of paintings that were to receive natural light from the encircling glass. A round service core that Wright called the "monitor" intersects the larger circle of the ramp on one side. He wanted the visitor to take the elevator up to the top and "drift down" the spiral to the open space on the ground. From there, the full ramp is visible, its drama culminating in the skylit dome. The building makes no bow to the neighboring apartment houses. Its free-standing sculpture establishes a powerful presence on Fifth Avenue facing Central Park, but the rounded contours suggest the "organic" nature of the park across the street. A block-long horizontal base on which the slightly receding cylinder appears to rest anchors its strong forms and establishes a relationship to the street and the site, at a mediating scale.

When construction was about to begin, the Department of Buildings found multiple violations and refused to issue a building permit — an old story to Wright, who consistently built without one. Since the violations could not be corrected without destroying the unusual structure and the open plan, help was sought from the all-powerful Robert Moses, then New York's building czar, who happened, conveniently, to be a relative of Wright's by marriage. Moses, an ultraconservative architecturally, had no love for the building, but the permit was issued without further delay. No builder could be found who wanted to brave the inevitable technical problems of the unprecedented construction, until former apprentice Edgar Tafel appeared with someone willing to take the challenge. Wright insisted on sharing credit on the cornerstone with the builder, George N. Cohen, who more than earned the recognition.

Wright got along well with Harry Guggenheim, Solomon's nephew, who headed the project after his uncle's death; another volume of cantankerous and amusing letters was added to Wright's growing collection. But Harry Guggenheim wanted no nonsense with theories and budgets; he delayed construction because of the high cost of building and shortages of materials after the war. There were design compromises and changes in program and policy. The museum was no longer dedicated to non-objective art or exclusively to Solomon Guggenheim's collection, nor would anything be displayed in the manner that had been envisioned. The family had long viewed Hilla Rebay as a lady Svengali whose power over Solomon extended from the paintings he purchased to the strange theories she espoused and the bizarre medical cures she recommended. She was removed as director and the penthouse apartment with a park view disappeared from the plans. A new board was established and a new director brought in, James Johnson Sweeney, who was violently opposed to every premise on which Wright's design was based; he made changes that sabotaged the building in every way possible.

Sweeney, who came from the Museum of Modern Art and had helped to establish its style and standards, did his best to remake the Guggenheim in that fashionable institution's image. The idea of a permanently fixed collection was dropped for a policy of acquisitions, diversity, and temporary exhibitions, although none of the necessary storage, preparation, or display space had been provided under the earlier program. Granted that the original concept was curious, and might have been even more curious in execution, the process of obliteration was brutal. Sweeney repainted Wright's soft ivory interiors stark white — Wright avoided and abhorred white — and substituted artificial light at the top of the ramp's outer walls. All this was done to create the kind of shadowless, neutral ambience favored by the modernists whom Wright had battled all his life. Sweeney ignored Wright's easel-like resting places and drove metal rods into the walls to suspend pictures far enough away from the distracting tilt and curve of the ramp to defeat the illusion that everything on it was off axis. At some point, the top of the spiral was shut for storage, amputating its ascent, hiding the domed skylight that was the climax of the design. But although Wright died before the Guggenheim's completion, he fought Sweeney to a draw from the grave, and Sweeney resigned in apoplectic frustration after a year in the job.

The building has continued to frustrate every director since, as each has tried to make peace with its demanding personality and physical challenges. What has survived, by default, is Wright's basic, powerful idea of unified space and structure. It has overridden the continuing controversies about its use and practicality, the indignities of antagonistic installations, two "restorations," and a brace of additions. Whatever the dramatic, spiraling interior lacks in flexibility for exhibition purposes — and the most serious charge leveled against it is that the architecture trumps the art — this soaring volume with its encircling ramps is an intensely moving experience. The impact is visual and visceral; it involves all the senses. The building is alive; the movement of people and their murmurous sound, the surrounding color and form, redefine social space and the way art is seen and felt within it, although certainly not as originally intended. It sets severe limitations; some art is instantly defeated, but some reaches remarkable heights. In the exhibition of Mark Rothko's abstractions, the paintings were seen simultaneously, ascending and descending the ramp, their luminous color glowing on many levels. The setting enlarged the perception of the work and the viewer's responses. With a bow to Emerson, and with some defensible hyperbole, you could even call the fusion of art and space transcendental.

While the Guggenheim was in construction, Wright made his New York headquarters in the Plaza hotel, Henry Hardenbergh's Beaux Arts dowager on Fifth Avenue at Fifty-ninth Street. Like his patron, Harry Guggenheim, he kept a permanent suite there, undisturbed by the discrepancy in their resources. True to form, he redecorated it to his own taste, with his own fabrics, colors, and objects, including his Japanese prints and the indispensable grand piano. He called it Taliesin East, entertaining extensively in his apartment and in the hotel's restaurants, and occasionally taking over the entire Palm Court; at one point, he saved the Palm Court from a disastrous "modernization." Also true to form, he may have neglected to pay the bills. He operated, as one observer said, without prudence or foresight, certain, as he so often repeated, that if the luxuries were acquired, the necessities would take care of themselves.

He made extravagant impulse purchases. Cash was spent immediately. Unable to pass up something wonderful in a gallery, he would use funds desperately needed to pay bills. Stopping in a Lincoln Continental showroom he ordered two cars, with special tops, in a custom color — his trademark Cherokee red — demanding instant delivery and letting it be known that he didn't expect to pay for them. He bought multiple Steinway pianos the same way. Only a master finagler could have operated on that lordly scale. His usual procedure when presented with an overdue account was to produce anything from a ten- to a hundred-dollar bill and finesse the rest. Someone would always step in to help, or he used well-cultivated gifts of denial and evasion.

In 1952, fire struck Taliesin for the third time — some say it was Wright's wiring, which, like his hydraulic engineering, occasionally failed, but this time it was part of the Hillside Home School buildings used by the Fellowship that was destroyed. Once more, he rebuilt, a repeated ritual that always meant changes, improvements, and a never-ending series of additions.

His eccentricities and his quick wit kept him constantly in the news. Never concerned about consistency or self-contradiction, he shamelessly expressed opinions on subjects he knew nothing about, convinced he had a direct line to the truth that bypassed the need for information. He was called a crackpot, or a genius, or both. Invited to give a talk at Yale for a student lecture series, where a number of missed signals had him threatening to leave immediately, he was described by one of the sponsors, Henry F. S. Cooper, as striding imperiously across the campus with cape flapping, cane twirling, "kicking pigeons out of the way."

In a TV "conversation" with Chicago poet and old friend Carl Sandburg in 1957, refereed by the suave British moderator Alistair Cooke, he was the complete contrarian and curmudgeon, disagreeing with everything said or suggested, but in a thoroughly entertaining way, holding out for the artist versus the scientist and heart over mind, while managing to punch out the Jefferson Memorial ("a classical comfort station"), the Washington Monument ("the act of an ignoramus . . . a point like a lead pencil"), and the skyscraper ("they make lumber out of steel . . . posts and beams tied together, like wood . . . and then they bring in the paperhanger and hang a façade on them. . . . There is a conspicuous, imperishable evidence of our inability to see the nature of anything from within"). "Wasn't there a great preacher lost in him?" asked Sandburg, hanging on the ropes. With a final kick, Wright consigned the skyscraper to the past, much as Hitchcock and Johnson had pigeonholed his problematic innovations a quarter of a century earlier. "I don't know why they consider that modern; that's nineteenth century; it's all nineteenth century," he said, relishing the hit.

He had already embraced the tall building, in his own way, in 1953. The twenty-story Price Company Tower in Bartlesville, Oklahoma, designed for Harold C. Price, a wealthy builder of oil and gas pipelines, was in an unlikely spot for a skyscraper, but it suited Wright's belief that tall buildings should stand in counterpoint to open land, enjoyed as highly visible works of art. Harold Price and his wife were another of those couples who appeared periodically and providentially to become loyal, indulgent client-patrons. The Price Tower was a completely unconventional concept of tall building construction, allowing Wright to revive a favorite, recurring idea that first appeared in his unrealized scheme for an apartment house for St. Mark's-in-the-Bouwerie in New York in 1928–1930. A taproot tower, structured like a tree, its central core was anchored by spreading, rootlike foundations, with the floors cantilevered like branches from the core. The building was a richly exuberant concrete polygram adorned with green copper spandrels and gold-tinted glass, with no two sides alike. When biographer Meryle Secrest visited it, she found it a delightful surprise "unaccountably deposited at a modest corner" in an unlikely town.

Even as Wright railed against big buildings and big cities, he unveiled his Mile High skyscraper for Chicago in 1956, a faceted, prismatic, tapering tower, presented in a spectacularly tall rendering, as beautiful as it was unbuildable. No one took it seriously except as a match for his own sky-high ego. Taste and technology have made extreme images familiar, but computer-aided architecture would produce no handsomer forms than those from Wright's unassisted imagination.

When he wasn't grandstanding, he called his sister Maginel, who had moved east with her husband, and begged for simple sustenance; she would bring a plain baked potato in a brown paper bag to his suite at the Plaza. In her memoir, *The Valley of the God-Almighty Joneses*, she marveled at her brother's energy; the endless new designs that he seemed to pour out kept the Taliesin studios working at fever pitch. When she asked how he managed it all, he expressed the fear that there wouldn't be time enough to get everything done. In

1949 and 1950 alone, he had received over 600 commissions, and more than a third of his total executed work was done in the last nine years of his life.

A major retrospective exhibition, "Sixty Years of Living Architecture," had its grand opening in Florence in 1951, and proceeded on an international tour to Zurich, Paris, Munich, Rotterdam, and Mexico City, arriving in New York in 1953, where Wright managed the coup of having it installed on the undeveloped site of the future Guggenheim Museum, along with a model Usonian house. He made his first and only trip to Wales, the land to which he was so deeply tied by family and temperament, in 1956. Invited to help "modernize" Iraq, he visited Baghdad in 1957, and then designed a cultural center that combined the unabashed romanticism of an *Arabian Nights* theme with a visionary act of urban planning. Mounded earthworks spiraled around the complex (the spiral again), recalling the circular plan of the ancient capital, while providing expandable ring roads for modern automobile traffic. The ambitious proposal was aborted by the coup that ended the Hashemite regime in 1958.

Wright turned ninety in 1957, although

he admitted only to a youthful eighty-eight. This was the year of his last great project, the Marin County Civic Center, in San Rafael, California, a conceptually brilliant scheme with bold, colorful imagery. His dedication to the generating force of the site and the nature of the land is stunningly evident in the plan — two long, arcaded wings of unequal length that bridge the hills, united by a domed rotunda. Wright used the logic of the structure's unique response to its physical setting to redefine the government building — instead of occupying vertically stacked office floors, the departments run horizontally, in balconied spaces with views. At ground level, roads go through the arcades, which support three glass-walled stories above. Arches, oculi, and metal sunscreens make repeated, rhythmic patterns, under gold-trimmed, aquamarine roofs. There are courts, fountains, and pools. The real Wright magic was not in the decorative details that caused the most comment, but in the way the building shatters convention for a solution of remarkable environmental amenity.

It has never been possible to deny the power and originality of Wright's architectural imagination, no matter what form it assumed, but much of his late work has remained a subject of controversy. He increasingly created a world of his own, full of bright color, exotic references, and futuristic imagery, with flying saucers, screens, spires, statues, and polychrome, jewel-like decoration, that is a curious mélange of Buck Rogers, the *Arabian Nights*, and Native American sources. Critics and historians who lavishly praised his earlier work found this decorative exuberance over the top. Neil Levine expresses the general view that it was "eccentric and unassimilable." Two of the most respected architectural writers of the 1970s, Manfredo Tafuri and Francesco dal Co, saw it as all downhill: a kind of "science fiction architecture" in which a "selfconscious exoticism" deteriorated to the level of "ultrakitsch."

But deviation from earlier norms and accepted practice into unfamiliar and often puzzling territory does not mean that an artist's powers have declined; in old age, the work tends to become freer and more experimental, less caring about expectations and conventions. When Picasso reworked the old masters in bold, personal interpretations, the paintings were considered by many to be a disappointing coda to his career. Late work is often treated as a form of senile decadence. Almost always problematic, it is often dismissed or discreetly ignored.

What disturbs us, and makes Wright's late work hard to accept, is that it is so uncool — so out of sync with contemporary sensibilities that favor an edgy minimalism, or a sophisticated tongue-in-cheek appropriation of the past. Wright's futurism is not the sleek, high-tech world of *The Matrix*; his references are too literal and sentimental for acceptable revisionist history. The crescent arches, rainbow fountains, and Aladdin statue of his Baghdad opera house, the tipis and clamshells of his churches and public buildings, the reds, blues, and golds, beads and balloons that adorned his late work, were increasingly at odds with a reductive twentieth-century aesthetic. Wright's personal sense of beauty was deeply rooted in the sentimental and religious beliefs of the nineteenth century that he never doubted or abandoned and continued to hold in defiant opposition to popular contemporary culture. He never lost his love of the exotic and the decorative — from the *Arabian Nights* scene he commissioned for the Oak Park Playroom and the narrative and mythical figures of the Midway Gardens, to the eternal feminine and metaphorical mystique of the statue *The Flower in the Crannied Wall.*

He was always out of the mainstream; he fit neither the Neue Sachlichkeit of the 1920s nor the age of irony with which the century ended. The only way he could be dealt with was to treat him as marginal, the outsider he claimed to be. With the breakdown of modernist rules and taboos, his historical and literary references became acceptable again. By the 1990s, Neil Levine defined his style as "a historicizing contextualism" — an architecture that seeks to express the uniqueness of a culture or the spirit of a place. This brought Wright back full circle to his early role as a revolutionary traditionalist, when he championed "the cause conservative," re-inventing everything in ways no one had imagined, embracing tradition while radically reconceiving it.

By ignoring convention, by denying prevailing taste and mores, by totally disassociating himself from the movements and institutions that dominated architecture in the twentieth century, he was free to be himself, to live, believe, and practice as he wished. At the same time that he proudly stressed his unrepentant individualism and never relinquished his sense of "otherness," he "rode the crest of the postwar acceptance of modern architecture with skill and flamboyance," in Levine's words, basking in his celebrity status. He had invented himself as the first of the "star" architects.

At the end of his life he simply indulged his powerful imagination and his obstinate taste for the pictorial and the sentimental of his Victorian mentors, given a space-age spin. His obsessive use of geometry, buildings straitjacketed by triangles, hexagons, and circles, turned into exercises of increasing, disorienting abstraction. Cataclysmic cultural changes took place over his long life span, but "truth against the world" positioned him stubbornly against them. He was a fascinating anachronism — a talented visionary and an unreconstructed romantic who produced design, planning, and structural concepts that the twenty-first century is still absorbing.

12

No one expected him to die. He had suffered from Ménière's disease in the 1950s, an inner ear problem with severe attacks of dizziness and nausea that would temporarily incapacitate him, but the rugged constitution established by those hardworking youthful years on Uncle James's farm sustained him, and his will to work never slackened. Easter 1959 had been celebrated, as usual, at Taliesin West, and elaborate plans were being made for a ninetieth birthday celebration in June; he would, of course, have been ninety-two. Lloyd brought news in March that Catherine had died recently, at eighty-seven. When Wright seemed saddened and disturbed that he had learned of her death after the funeral took place, Lloyd wondered why, since he had cared so little for her in life, he should care about her in death. Ten days later, on Saturday, April 4, he developed abdominal pains and was taken to a hospital in Phoenix. Surgery was performed for an abdominal obstruction the following Monday, and he seemed to be recovering, but on Thursday, April 9, suddenly and quietly, he died.

The funeral took place in Wisconsin, and the burial was in the Lloyd Jones family graveyard. Meryle Secrest's biography gives the most complete account of what followed. Wes Peters, Wright's son-in-law and primary assistant, told how Wright's body was put on a pickup truck by the Fellowship, and driven back to Wisconsin, for twenty-eight hours without stopping, a distance of 1,800 miles. The flower-filled coffin rested in front of the great Taliesin fireplace on a drape of Cherokee red velvet. This was the only time, Wright's son Lloyd recalled later, that he realized his father was a small man.

On Sunday, April 12, the coffin was placed on a horse-drawn wagon and driven from the house to the chapel. Olgivanna followed with their daughter, Iovanna, along with family and friends. After a simple ceremony, with readings from the Bible and Emerson, he was buried. In announcements of his death, it was noted that the burial was temporary; Wright's body would be moved to a new chapel he had designed as his last resting place and memorial, to be built close to the family's

Unity Chapel, the Silsbee building Wright had assisted on so many years ago. The building's footings had been established, stone cut and brought to the site from a neighboring quarry, and Wright had supervised the planting of trees for the approach. But work had stopped, with nothing more done in the previous two years as the Fellowship became increasingly established in Arizona and trips were made less often to Wisconsin. And so the situation remained for another twenty-six years — until Olgivanna died, on March 1, 1985.

In death, as in life, Wright was a magnet for scandal; he was not to rest in peace. Olgivanna's dying wish, reported by her doctor, had been that her husband and her daughter Svetlana by her first marriage, Wes Peters's wife, who had been killed in an automobile accident many years before, be exhumed and cremated, and their ashes brought to Arizona to be buried with hers, in a memorial garden to be created for the purpose. Such was the strength of her hold on the Fellowship that she had run since Wright's death, and so uncompromising the loyalty demanded and delivered under her matriarchal rule, that no one questioned the propriety or appropriateness of her final request. None of this was in her will, but she appears to have spoken about it in the years before she died. According to her daughter Iovanna, her wishes needed only to be expressed to be carried out. Even in death, they could not be ignored; Wes Peters explained that her orders had the aura of Holy Writ. Apparently no one opposed the procedure. But the fact that the ghoulish undertaking was carried out with the greatest haste and in the strictest secrecy suggests that some doubts might have been entertained.

And so began the most incredible, posthumous chapter of Wright's far from tranquil life. Again, a hegira, as Wright always called the trip between the two Taliesins — with a long, frantic trip by members of the Fellowship to bring back Wright's remains, as commanded, although the logistics of doing so for Olgivanna's long-deceased daughter presented obstacles that quietly removed it from the agenda.

The necessary paperwork for the removal of Wright's body had been done by Iovanna, but the chapel's custodian was not notified and the digging was done hurriedly, leaving the disturbed grave unrestored. The body was cremated immediately, with the coroner sworn to secrecy, and the ashes taken back to Arizona. But the news got out, and the *Madison Capital Times* published the story, to a crescendo of protest. In an expression of collective outrage, the Wisconsin Legislature passed a resolution condemning the removal of Wright's body; it was viewed as an act of vandalism. The writer and editor Karl E. Meyer, whose family had been close to Wright, likened the macabre switch from Wisconsin to Arizona to "uprooting Jefferson from Monticello for reburial in Beverly Hills." When Wright's other children learned what had happened, they were incensed, calling it "grave-robbing" and "desecration." It seemed obvious to everyone that Wright's roots were with the Lloyd Joneses in the valley, in the gentle rolling hills and farmland of Taliesin that he loved. He had always come back, through tragedy and adversity, rebuilding Taliesin and his life each time.

In Arizona, Olgivanna had played a central role; they had built Taliesin West together, and in the years after Wright's death, she reigned supreme, overseeing a Gurdjieff-like commune. The Wisconsin Taliesin belonged to his past; it was the house he had built for Mamah, his great love, and now he was with her eternally in death, where he had buried her seventy years before. This must have been anathema to Olgivanna, his companion of thirty-four years, survivor of a marriage that had begun in shared misfortunes and become a union of mutual dependence and loyalty. It was she who had made the Fellowship a reality, who solved its problems day by day; he had always ceded the management and authority to her. She had established a life of stability for him. Like his habit of acquiring the luxuries and letting the necessities take care of themselves, he acquired the women who saw to it that the necessities were procured. He accepted their arrangements, and one wonders if he might not even have accepted this one.

The announcement was made that a joint interment would take place within six months. Nothing happened for several years, while the ashes remained somewhere at Taliesin West. Eventually, the memorial garden was built in Arizona and a reburial ceremony held. By this time, the Fellowship had established itself as the permanent guardian of Wright's legacy. Under the leadership of Wes Peters, the Fellowship, as Taliesin Associated Architects, continued to carry out Wright's unbuilt plans, assisting and advising on preservation and renovation, and accepting commissions for new work in the Wright spirit and style. But without Wright's sensitive eye and the inventiveness that was constantly breaking new ground, the work became formulaic. The Frank Lloyd Wright Archives, under Bruce Brooks Pfeiffer, with the Frank Lloyd Foundation, took on the monumental task of organizing and preserving the massive amount of archival material and personal memorabilia of Wright's life. One of the surprising finds after Olgivanna's death was a trunk stuffed with rare Japanese fabrics, crumpled and forgotten.

While Olgivanna controlled the archives, access was restricted; permission was given selectively, and high fees were charged. There was a noticeable resistance to criticism or any breach of the Wright legend. Under Pfeiffer's direction, the drawings, documents, and artifacts, all desperately in need of attention, were organized, preserved, and made available for research. With the opening of the archives, a new era of Wright scholarship began. The 1980s and '90s became active decades of rediscovery and reappraisal, enriched by a steady stream of documentary publications authored by Pfeiffer drawn from Wright's letters and records. As books and exhibitions multiplied, a virtual Wright industry was born. In 1994, the Museum of Modern Art presented a comprehensive retrospective of Wright's career.

H. Allen Brooks, a Wright editor and historian, concluded many years ago that Wright was "too elusive, too profound, to be easily explained." In the text of an earlier show at the museum, culled from 8,000 drawings in the Taliesin archives, Arthur Drexler called Wright "one of the most original architects in all of history," an innovator with a "lyrical vision," whose ideas were "still new, still relevant, and often untried."

He led an imperfect life, often indulging in self-destructive behavior. Some of his troubles were of his own making; others would have crushed a lesser man. He survived everything, an architectural Don Quixote battling against contemporary reality for his stubbornly held version of an elusive truth. In his mind, the ends always justified the means; any behavior was permissible if it served his art and the lifestyle he thought he deserved. His buildings, like his life, were flawed, conceptually so far ahead of current practice and technology that their failures provided deathless ammunition for the legion of Wright myth breakers. Perfection was not his game. Part of the beauty of Wright's work, Arthur Drexler observed, "is the release it offers from the idea of perfection. His architecture, like life itself, renders perfection irrelevant . . . every event has significance, but there is no final event, no perfect answer; history cannot come to an end." What remains at the heart of it is its humanity, its search for connections with our world and our lives.